A Family Secret

My shocking true story of surviving a childhood in hell

MAUREEN WOOD

WITH JOE AND ANN CUSACK

HARPER
element

Certain details in this story, including names, places and dates, have been changed to protect privacy.

HarperElement
An imprint of HarperCollins*Publishers*
1 London Bridge Street
London SE1 9GF

www.harpercollins.co.uk

HarperCollins*Publishers*
1st Floor, Watermarque Building, Ringsend Road
Dublin 4, Ireland

First published by HarperElement 2020

1 3 5 7 9 10 8 6 4 2

© Maureen Wood 2020

Maureen Wood asserts the moral right to
be identified as the author of this work

A catalogue record of this book is
available from the British Library

ISBN 978-0-00-844156-2

Printed and bound in Great Britain by
CPI Group (UK) Ltd, Croydon

MIX
Paper from
responsible sources
FSC™ C007454

This book is produced from independently certified FSC™ paper
to ensure responsible forest management.

For more information visit: www.harpercollins.co.uk/green

A Family Secret

This book is dedicated to my angel baby Christopher and to all the silent victims of abuse. I hope it helps them find their voice.

Prologue

No doubt about it, this was how the other half lived. Leaning back in my seat, feet up, sipping my drink, I felt on top of the world. Which, of course, I was.

Peering through the gap beside my seat, I watched my children, *almost* all my children, in the row behind, chatting and buzzing, intoxicated with a mix of holiday euphoria and that peculiar strain of exhaustion that travelling brings.

'I can't wait to go to Harry Potter World,' Naomi was saying. 'Imagine walking down Diagon Alley!'

I smiled. They deserved a treat, that was for sure.

And then, with a sudden whoosh, like a wind beneath the plane, I was hurtling back through time, peering through another gap, watching another of my children. The one who had made all this possible. The one who was missing today.

* * *

It was already sunny at 5.45 a.m. that July morning when Louise arrived to collect me. I was ready, pacing the living room, my nerves stretched and taut. I didn't say a word on the journey there; it felt respectful to travel in silence. And then, as we pulled up, I saw the glare of floodlights and the white tent around my baby son's resting place. We had been given strict Home Office instructions that we were not allowed inside the cemetery. But there was no way I could stay away. He was mine, my boy.

We had been instructed to park across the road, so that we didn't draw attention to the cemetery. But I had a good view from out of the car window and I watched, appalled yet transfixed, through a gap in the cemetery railings as the digging began. Forensic officers in white space suits waited, like Martian pallbearers, for my Christopher, my baby, to surface. And then, there he was; his tiny coffin looked almost like a toy from where I was standing.

'Mummy is sorry,' I whispered. 'I'm so sorry, Christopher.'

As his coffin was lifted into a plain grey van, I remembered the innocence in his wide blue eyes, I smelled the newness of his skin, I felt his tiny, delicate fingers curling around my thumb. And I was overwhelmed with a tsunami of loss and despair. My poor bruised heart ached and wept to see him again. Off went the van, carrying my precious cargo. Carrying my hopes, my heartbreak and the distant promise of peace.

A Family Secret

Christopher had saved me once, and now, twenty-five years on, I was asking him to save me again. My guardian angel was risen from the dead, bringing with him my chance for justice.

Chapter 1

'This,' said my mother Maureen, 'is your new stepdad.'

She took a step back on the station platform to admire him herself before singling me out for a glare.

'Well?' she snapped. 'Where are your manners? Say hello.'

But I took one long look at his orangey-brown hair and his thin, mean face and I recoiled. My knuckles were white as I gripped my suitcase, my eyes staring, downcast, at the chewing gum ground into the platform tiles.

'Hello,' I mumbled.

My mother slipped her arms around him and smiled, and we all trailed behind them, dragging our cases with aching arms and aching hearts. Away from the station, away from all we knew, and off to yet another new life.

I could barely remember the last time I'd seen my mother before this. She and my biological father, John Donnelly, had separated when I was just a toddler. And on Boxing Day 1975, Mum dumped my older brother,

Jock, and me, with our paternal grandparents, William and Eliza Donnelly. She didn't visit us, as far as I know, and she didn't even check on us. I was just five years old. And yet I was quite happy without my mother; my grandparents were warm and kind and made sure we wanted for nothing. I have vague memories, too, of an aunt painting my toenails and playing house with me. Because I was the smallest, the whole family made such a fuss of me.

But later that year we were taken into care, to live in a Catholic children's home called Nazareth House, in Glasgow. There we were reunited with our other two sisters, both older than me. It was nice to be back with my siblings, but I missed the easy affection of my grandparents' home. The timetable at Nazareth House was strict, almost military. The home was run by nuns who, it seemed to me, chatted very little and smiled even less. We were up early every morning to say prayers, then we had to be dressed, fed and in chapel, on our knees, by 8 a.m. By the time we got to school I was already exhausted. After school there were more prayers, food, chores, then bed. We were woken at midnight for a last trip to the loo, to ensure we didn't wet the bed. Nobody misbehaved or stepped out of line – there was simply no scope for it in a place like that. We were under the watchful, beady eyes of the nuns all the time.

I was in a large girls' dormitory with my sisters. We had a narrow single bed each with a miserably thin mattress, and a small bedside cupboard to store all the possessions that we didn't have. The boys' dormitories were along another corridor, and they sat in a different area of the dining hall, too, so we rarely saw our big brother, Jock. We saw Mum very rarely at the children's home, nor our dad, apart from one single visit, who now seemed consigned to history. We wouldn't see him again for many years.

As I recount the facts now, it sounds like a pitiful and wretched existence, and yet it was quite the opposite. I liked being in the home. Perversely, I preferred the rigidity and the predictability there to the uncertainty and chaos I associated with my mother. At Nazareth House I was at least fed and warm. The nuns were firm and austere, but as I settled in there I realised too that they were always fair and reasonable. I never felt as though I was singled out in any way. I never felt picked on or ostracised or bullied. Life was tough, of course it was, but it was tough for us all. We were all in the same boat, and there was a comfort in the collective hardship. There was a togetherness and a camaraderie with the other girls, and though we didn't have birthday cakes or bedtime stories or new shoes we had each other. There were plenty of giggles; chasing each other down the long corridors, tickling each other when we were supposed to be praying in Mass, or telling ghost stories in the midnight gloom of the long dormitories to scare each other half to death. I really was happy enough, day to day, in my little routine. There was a security and a feeling of safety about the place that I clung to. And though I didn't know it then, the children's home, with the chilly dormitory and the strict and distant nuns, would be the last place I would feel safe for a very long time. I knew where I was with the nuns. I knew where I was supposed to be at every hour of every day. And for a small child, such certainty is golden. I would only appreciate that, of course, after it was snatched away.

Three years later, in 1978, my mother arrived, without warning, to take us back out of care and into the new life she had fashioned for herself, and which she expected us to fall into without complaint.

'Come on now,' she said, clapping her hands as we walked out of the children's home and into the sunshine. 'We've a long journey ahead.'

Stepping onto the train at the station in Glasgow, I felt a ripple of both excitement and anxiety. The train itself was thrilling – whizzing past towns I'd never even heard of, giving me snapshot glimpses of what life I had been missing whilst I had been cocooned behind the huge doors of Nazareth House.

When we got off the train, in Stoke-on-Trent, our new stepfather, John Wood, was waiting. We had a little brother, too. It was all change, all different.

Our new home was a three-bedroomed semi on a long and busy street in a suburb close to the town centre. We settled in quickly because we had to. We soon picked up that Mum was not someone who liked her patience tested. She worked in a pub and John Wood was a miner, so they were often out of the house until late in the evening, and this gave us the perfect opportunity to run riot.

It was the summer holidays of 1978 when we arrived, so we had no school. All structure, all routine, was abandoned, and we went wild. The feeling of having nothing to do and nobody to answer to was at once exhilarating and frightening. I was seven years old, and I felt like I'd broken free.

At first, all five of us kids slept in a double bed until the new furniture arrived. Then I shared a bunk bed with one of my sisters – I had the bottom bunk, and though it got me into trouble, my blankets were always crumpled and messy.

'Why can't you keep yourself tidy like your sisters?' Mum complained. 'You're always the problem. Always.'

I loved to pull threads out of the pink bedspread that covered my blankets. It earned me a thick ear from Mum when she saw the strands all over the floor, but it was a nervous habit and I just couldn't help myself.

We each had a set of rosary beads on the bedside table and we prayed every night. I looked forward to Mass on Sundays; Mum didn't go to church, but I would happily go by myself. I enjoyed the familiarity and the reassuring routine of the service; it reminded me of Nazareth House.

Mum worked long hours, but when she was home there was discipline and order. We all ate together, in a heavy silence, around a large pine table. After tea we were allowed to go out to play in the street.

'Until the streetlamps are lit!' my mother would shout. 'And no later!'

There was a load of local kids our age, and we formed straggling, giggling teams, with mass games of tig and football. We played rounders on a big field behind the estate or 'two ball' against the back wall of the house.

'If I hear that ball one more time, I'll slap you so hard you won't sit down for a month,' Mum would yell.

We couldn't see her, but we could imagine her, hand on hip, waggling the obligatory finger, her face screwed up in anger. We sniggered, with the safety of a brick wall between us, and waggled our fingers back for good effect. I made a best pal, Joanne, who lived just across the street. She and I would play skipping or hold imaginary tea parties for our beloved dollies on the pavement. As we grew more adventurous we'd play 'Knock-a-door-run' on houses further up the street. It would take us ages to pluck up courage to tap on the first door, but after we had done so it was strangely addictive and we would run along the entire row of houses, knocking on each door and then running away, helpless with laughter, as the occupants swore and shouted after our disappearing heads. There was one occasion when a woman chased us along the street in her slippers, and we hid behind a hedge and chuckled as she shouted furiously for us to show ourselves. Another time, one of the neighbours set the hosepipe on us for knocking on his door. Again, we ended up guffawing in a heap behind some dustbins. I was never the ringleader; I was a shy kid and

6

I would generally follow the older ones into trouble, but I enjoyed every minute of it. There was nothing funnier to us kids than winding up adults and watching them blow, like fireworks.

The days were long and sunny, and we had lots to be happy about. We were well fed and well dressed – Mum always made sure of that. We had a little dog, Nipper, and a cat called Toots. To the outside world we were a run-of-the-mill, average sort of family. Later in the evenings, before bed, we'd all gather in the long living room that ran the length of the house, with a coal fire in the middle. Coal was free and plentiful, because of John Wood's job down the mine, so we had physical warmth, at least. The rest, we could do nothing about.

Starting school that September was tough. That first day my stomach swirled with excitement and trepidation. We had strong Scottish accents, which I'd already discovered were not always that popular in Stoke-on-Trent. And when I stood up in class to say my name, I might as well have been speaking in Swahili.

'What did she say?' shouted one kid. 'Sounds like mumbo-jumbo to me.'

The teacher, probably trying to help the situation, asked me where I was born. But she would only make matters worse.

'Germany,' I replied. 'My dad was in the army.'

There was a chorus of jeers and boos around the classroom.

'So you're a Kraut!' they shouted in delight. 'A Nazi!'

I tried to explain that I'd moved to Scotland when I was a baby and had no memory at all of my time in Germany. But that didn't make any difference at all.

'We've got the enemy standing here in Stoke-on-Trent!' they laughed. 'Lock her in the cleaning cupboard.'

Most of the kids let the joke go after that first day, but one boy in particular was vile. He nicknamed me Hitler, and it lasted all through school. Every time I walked past him he would dig me in the arm or do a Nazi salute.

For months I kept myself to myself and I had very few friends. Instead, I sought solace in books. I spent my playtimes and lunchtimes reading Enid Blyton and Clive King. Even in the playground I'd sit on the tarmac, with my face buried in a *Famous Five* novel. I could lose myself completely in a far-fetched adventure, slipping into the role of my favourite characters, transported to another town, another story, another life. My favourite character was George, a tomboy who was always getting herself embroiled in trouble. She was brave and fiery, too, and probably a little bit of me was envious of her. As I turned each page I felt every victory, every disappointment, everything. I was a loner, quite a solitary kid, and it wasn't just because of the bullies and the new school. By nature I enjoyed being on my own. I was quite happy with my own company. And, of course, there was nothing wrong with that. But I look back now and wonder whether that is why I was targeted. Whether that is why it all began.

My mother and John Wood were married at Newcastle-under-Lyme register office and afterwards they had a reception in the local pub where Mum worked. It was a great party; I remember I had a new dress and I was allowed to invite some of my pals from the street. I stayed up later than I'd ever been allowed. From that day we all called John Wood 'Dad'. It was expected, and we didn't question it or object. We fell into line. All, that was, except Jock.

'You're not my dad,' Jock told him angrily. 'And you never will be.'

Jock was twelve, five years older than me, and already surging with hormones and aggression. He made it clear, right from the start, that he hated Dad. Jock was fiercely loyal to our natural dad, whom he remembered far more clearly, and with much more affection, than I did. There were regular flare-ups between Jock and Dad. Jock refused to do what Dad said and regularly swore at him, and unless Mum was in the house he did just as he pleased.

'You can't tell me what to do,' he said angrily. 'You've no right.'

Dad was only 5 foot 7 and not particularly well-built, and although Jock was not yet taller than him he seemed to tower above him. Mentally, at least, he had the edge. In one argument, Dad broke his own hand trying to punch Jock, when he ended up hitting the wall instead. Mum punched Jock black and blue for his bad behaviour, so violently he probably wished he had the broken hand instead. To the rest of us it was seen as quite a comical incident, and we would snigger every time we passed the dent in the wall.

I stayed well out of the way of all the trouble. I liked peace and quiet, and when I was inside I spent most of my spare time reading. I'd often hide myself away, in the still of the bedroom, engrossed in my latest book, whilst all hell let loose downstairs. Dad himself was a keen reader, too.

'You can travel the world in a book,' he used to say. 'Get away from it all.'

It was just about the only thing he and I had in common. He enjoyed the odd classic, *Oliver Twist* and *Great Expectations*, which he passed on to me. But mostly he read books on horror and crime. It did not bode well for the future, and later I would look back and shudder at the irony.

Dad would often treat himself to a new paperback, especially if he had time off work, but I was never allowed to buy a book. All my reading material came from school or from the local library. Aside from his love of books, which didn't really fit with the rest of his character, Dad was a straightforward, no-nonsense sort of bloke. And unless he was dealing with Jock, he was a quiet and taci-turn character; Mum did most of the shouting in our house. But the notion of escape, of broadening my horizons, through a novel really appealed to me. And the seclusion, as I read on my own, hour after hour, was bliss. My usual nickname was 'Mo-Jo' but Mum gave me the nickname 'Dozy-Mosey' too, because I was forever tripping up as I walked around the house with my nose in a book.

I loved having a nickname. Mum rarely showed me any attention and never much affection either. She was not a tactile person, and not given to easy shows of emotion. So her choosing a nickname for me was a small sign that she had noticed me and that I figured, to some degree at least, in her thoughts. It gave me a feeling of belonging and I grasped it with both hands.

Apart from the bust-ups between Dad and Jock, it was Mum who doled out the discipline in the family. She had a fearsome temper, and her punishments, more often than not, were brutal. When we got up in the morning we had to tiptoe around the house, speaking in whispers. Waking Mum was like waking the devil; she would hit the roof if her lie-in was interrupted. One morning I woke her by shouting at one of my sisters. Mum marched downstairs, her eyes blazing with fury, and whacked me across the knee with a poker. Over forty years on, I still have the scar.

Whilst our lives were in some ways chaotic, spent running around outside with droves of other kids, they were strangely regimented, too. We had lists of chores to carry out: hoovering the bedrooms, changing the beds, dusting, polishing, washing and ironing. And Mum was always handy with her fists if our efforts weren't up to scratch. To me, she was a bit like a dormant World War 2 bomb, lurking upstairs. One false move and she could explode, at any time.

We had a rota taped to the pantry door and all chores had to be carried out straight after school. If we went out to play without finishing them first, we had Mum to answer to.

One day, much to our amusement, Jock simply refused to do his tasks.

'If you want the bathroom cleaning, do it your fucking self,' he told my mother.

We watched, transfixed and delighted, as she grabbed him by the throat and rammed him up against the wall. She was only 5 foot 2 tall, plump, with a round face and glasses, but she was more than a match for Jock.

'You will do as you're told or I will fucking kill you!' she seethed, her hand on her hip.

I was scared, but I was used to being scared, so it was no big deal. There was an undercurrent of fear and uncertainty in the house all the time, and I just got used to it. Another time, Mum had told me to change the beds, but I was only eight years old and getting a pillow back into a pillowcase proved much harder than I had anticipated.

'Do I have to do everything, you dumb bitch?' she spat.

She cracked me hard against the back of my head before grabbing the pillow from me. I shrugged it off and quickly learned how to do my chores to her standards. But what I really wanted was to learn how to cook. Even as a little girl I enjoyed being in the kitchen; we had a large ceramic sink and a wooden drainer and an old black cooker. To me, it felt like the warmest and friendliest room in the house. Mum was a good cook, too; she enjoyed baking and trying new recipes.

'Can I help?' I asked, poking my face round the door of the kitchen.

But Mum flew at me as though I'd done something wrong.

'Get out of my bloody kitchen!' she shouted, swatting me with a tea towel. 'Don't ever come in here again.'

Again, I sauntered off without giving it much thought. I was used to her. Yet after she had finished cooking she always called us in to wash up and clear away her mess. My sister washed, and I dried. The shared hardship might have brought about a camaraderie, a sense of togetherness, but somehow it drove a wedge between us kids, and our chores were done in silence, under the watchful, waiting eye of our mother.

But if I was wary of my parents, I idolised Jock. He was my big brother and I looked up to him and loved him with all my heart. Of all my siblings, he and I were the closest. To me, he was the tallest, strongest, bravest brother I could have wished for. And I was indulgent of his moods and his grumpiness, too. I knew he reserved the worst of his temper for Dad.

One day I was walking home, glued to my Enid Blyton book as usual, and one of the older boys from my school started to make fun of me.

'You're a swot,' he teased. 'What a nerd, always stuck in a book.'

And with that he punched me in the face and my nose just exploded. There was blood everywhere. Gasping with pain, I ran home sobbing, blood staining my school uniform. As soon as Jock saw me he demanded an explanation, before grabbing his leather jacket and going out to find the offender.

'I battered him,' he told me later, in a matter-of-fact manner. 'He won't be bothering you again. Don't worry, Mo-Jo.'

Jock didn't make a big fuss about it; he was well-known for fighting and getting into trouble in our neighbourhood and the other kids were terrified of him. It was no big deal for him to be throwing punches. He was a big lad with an even bigger attitude. The next day I spotted the same boy as I walked to school, and he ran off in alarm. He never even looked my way again. I played it cool, but secretly I was beaming and bursting with pride. I felt completely untouchable. My Jock, my protector, had laid down the law.

But whether Jock really did it for me or simply for his own amusement, I would never know. I didn't give it much thought at that age. I just felt as though I had someone on my side for once, and it felt fantastic. But though I was in awe of Jock, I never wanted to be like

A Family Secret

him. I marvelled at him, but I did not admire him. I think I sensed, even then, that he had hidden depths and they might well be swirling with filth. But for now he was a typically wayward teenager. He wore a uniform of skinny jeans, a white T-shirt, Doc Marten boots, and spent most of his time in his bedroom, with the Sex Pistols blaring out and Mum hollering up the stairs at him.

'Turn that crap off!' she screamed.

It wasn't until she was hammering on his door, ready for a fist fight, that he complied. Sometimes he took it even further than that, and he would wait until she was battering him before he gave in. One day he came home from the barbers smirking and with a shocking Mohican and, again, Mum flew into a rage.

'What will people think?' she screamed.

But Jock didn't seem to care at all. He was in regular trouble, and he took it all in his stride. Authority – and the threat of authority – never seemed to bother him one bit. I wondered whether really he quite enjoyed all the fuss.

Although I didn't have many friends at school I had lots of mates on our street. Joanne and I were part of a much larger group and there was often a big gang of us playing manhunt on the field behind the houses, or swimming up at the local pond. One time I fell off a rope swing into the pond, and after that I learned to swim pretty quickly. Now, even though I was just eight years old, I loved splashing around and diving in with the bigger kids.

Our local lollipop lady, Jane, had a heart of gold, and she would often pack a big picnic for us all on sunny days. One July day, at the start of the 1979 summer holidays, was a real scorcher, so hot the tarmac was bubbling up on the road outside. The street was swarming with wasps and kids; we were the only ones with any energy in the baking heat. There were mums in deckchairs outside their front doors, fanning themselves with rolled-up newspapers. There were dads with hankies on their heads and socks on, knocking back cans and gearing themselves up for a brawl later on.

'Water fight! Water fight!' screamed one of the boys.

And that was all it took. Word spread through the kids like an electric shock and suddenly we were all racing down the street to fill old Fairy liquid bottles with water. Our water supply was temperamental in the house, because of the summer drought, so we had to queue to use an outside tap further up the street. Seconds later it was all-out war. We raced up and down the paths, hiding behind fences and bins, squealing in horrified delight when we were sprayed with ice-cold water.

It was the best and the worst of shocks, all at the same time. But as the heat began to fade I found myself soaked to the skin and ready for a hot bath. Our home-made weapons discarded for another day, we all trooped inside, glowing with the excitement of the fight, shivering with the cold.

As I went upstairs I could hear Pink Floyd blasting out of Jock's bedroom. His door was closed, as always. He was too cool and too angry for water fights. I slipped into the bathroom, closed the door behind me, and stripped down to my undies. To my surprise, the door opened again and there was Jock, standing right behind me.

'What do you want?' I said, hugging my arms around myself, suddenly self-conscious.

He didn't speak. Instead, he leaned towards me, put his hand down my knickers and started to touch me. I was scared and anxious. It didn't feel right, but I didn't know what it was. Fear overwhelmed me and, though I tried to shrink back, he just pushed himself further into me.

'Stop,' I pleaded, my voice wavering. 'Please, stop.'

It felt like a lifetime before Jock took his hand away. He looked me in the eye and said: 'If you breathe a word, we will all go back into care, and it will all be your fault.'

He stomped back to his room without saying anything more and I was left, shivering now with shock, wondering what on earth had just taken place. Suddenly nauseous, I ran to my bedroom, slammed the door, and cried on my bed for hours.

When Mum came in, she tutted impatiently and said, 'What are you crying for? What's the matter, for God's sake? Shut the bloody noise up now.'

I shook my head and said truthfully, 'I don't know. I really don't know.'

'Well, I'll give you something to cry about if you don't stop,' she snapped.

Maureen Wood

I had no name for what had happened to me. And even if I had, I couldn't have confided in her. She just wasn't that sort of mother. I had the responsibility, too, of keeping the rest of my family safe, for hadn't Jock threatened that we would all go back into care if I told anyone? Instead, I pushed it to the back of my mind, convinced it was a one-off, some sort of aberration in Jock that he would not repeat. And when I saw him the next day he acted completely normally. I could almost imagine it had never happened in the first place.

It was a couple of weeks later that Mum sent us out blackberry picking, so that she could bake a pie. She was a walking contradiction; on the one hand, she would attack us for the slightest transgression, yet she would also bake and cook wonderful meals and insist that we all ate around the table together at 5 p.m. each night. And again, we were left to our own devices, fighting and running wild. Yet there were also things expected of us; we had responsibilities. She was impossible to predict, and that made her all the more tricky to deal with.

On this particular day we were packed off to Black Bank, an area near our house that was famous for plump blackberries. The path took us past the pond, through ferns and grasses to a large banking. To me, as a little girl, it was like a forbidden forest. There was a whole gang of us from the street searching out the best berries. It was like a day out. But as we picked and chatted I

18

suddenly noticed Jock creeping up behind us. And then he grabbed my arm and steered me into the ferns, away from everyone, where it was quiet. None of my friends even looked around, but of course they all knew Jock, so they presumed he just wanted to talk to me. Besides, they knew his reputation, too, and none of them would have dared question him. I could feel his nails digging into my flesh. My heart was in my mouth. I felt my insides churning.

'What are you doing?' I asked.

But my voice was smaller and thinner than I'd hoped. I was no match for him. Once we were away from the others, he pushed me heavily onto the grass, lay down beside me, and pulled up my skirt. I screwed up my eyes and held my breath as he forced my knickers down and thrust a finger roughly inside me.

'You're hurting me!' I squealed. 'Leave me alone! Please, Jock, stop. Please!'

'I'm enjoying it too much,' he grunted.

I tried pushing him off, but he was too strong. His breathing was loud, rasping and uneven. He didn't even look like Jock. My Jock. In my child's mind he looked like a monster, a ghoul, a bogeyman, and nothing like my brother at all. On the other side of the brambles, I could hear the rest of the kids laughing and playing. But they might as well have been on the other side of the world, they were so out of reach. For me, it lasted hours. In reality it was a matter of a few minutes. When he was finished, Jock just got up and walked away. With shaking hands, I pulled my knickers up, the long grass itching my legs, as the tears streamed down my face.

I couldn't face the other children, so I stumbled off in the other direction, my thoughts clouded by the physical agony Jock had inflicted. I felt like I was burning inside. But I eventually detoured back to get some blackberries, because knew I would be in trouble if I went home empty-handed.

To a little girl, a beating from my mother and a sexual assault by my brother were both much the same. I was too young and too innocent to understand the distinction. I knew simply that they brought pain, and I would try to avoid them at all costs. Afterwards I made my way home, but the attack dominated my thoughts. It never occurred to me to tell anyone, though; Mum was not someone I could approach. I knew that from bitter experience.

I had once come home from school crying because another child had hit me. Instead of the sympathy I was kidding myself she might show, Mum had shouted:

'Get out there and belt them back or I will give you a good hiding. And stop crying, for God's sake. Your face will stick like that if you're not careful.'

So I knew it was pointless to ask her for help.

The blackberry pie stuck in my throat like shards of glass as we sat around the table in silence. Jock didn't even look at me, but then, he never usually did. He kept himself to himself. As time went on, I managed, once again, to shut it out. I still didn't know what it was. I didn't have a way out either, so the only option open to me was to block it out entirely. I no longer felt safe with Jock. But he was still my brother, and I still loved him. I couldn't change that, whether I wanted to or not.

Chapter 2

I have no idea whether my ninth birthday, in October 1979, was a happy one, because now the memory has been completely destroyed in my mind. There was certainly no party, and the day would have been spent pretty much like any other: ticking off a seemingly endless list of chores before playing out with the other kids in the street. But part way through a game of rounders Mum called me inside and gestured at the radio.

'Hush,' she ordered. 'Just listen.'

We sat and waited for a few moments and then the DJ on Radio Stoke said: 'And now a very Happy Birthday to Maureen Donnelly.'

My face lit up as he began to play 'Bright Eyes' by Art Garfunkel.

I was thrilled. Mum was not a demonstrative woman and I knew better than to hug her, but I felt so pleased. More than anything, I felt special. As if I was noticed, loved and wanted. I ran back outside to my friends, bubbling over with my news, that I was so important I had my very own birthday dedication on the radio.

'Honestly,' I told them. 'He said my name. My full name.'

By the evening I was lying on my bed, reading quietly in the now-empty house. The day's events were still warm in my memory when Jock padded quietly into the room.

'Happy Birthday,' he smiled. 'Have you had a nice day?'

There was a moment of anxiety when he came through the door, followed by confusion. He was smiling and seemed so unthreatening. Had he forgotten the attack, just as I had tried to? Perhaps it was something he hadn't wanted to do and now he was sorry? Whatever the truth of it, I felt sure it was in the past. It was done with now. Besides, it was two months ago, and that was a lifetime to a nine-year-old. What I realise now, with hindsight, is that Jock had simply been biding his time. Waiting to see if I would tell anyone. Waiting for the house to be empty. Waiting to pounce.

Jock sat on the bed and said: 'I've got your present here. It's a special birthday present.'

Excited, I let my book fall and said, 'What is it?'

Without another word, Jock unzipped his trousers and I watched, frozen with horror, as his face clouded over, and once again he no longer looked like my brother. It was as though someone had drawn a dark blind over his real features. The monster was back. He pulled his penis out of his trousers and said: 'This is the present.'

And then he raped me. Pain, a searing, cruel, unforgiving pain, deluged throughout my entire body. I felt like I had been stabbed. I stared, wide-eyed, at the flowery pink and purple curtains, at the pink bed covers, at the Abba posters above my sister's bed. I remembered how Mum went mad when I unpicked the pink bedspreads and I imagined myself now, picking at threads, pulling out strands, one after another, faster and faster, whilst my brother raped me. He wore a St Christopher necklace and it swung back and forth, back and forth, like a pendulum, as he thrusted back and forth inside me. I fixed on the necklace, trying to blot out everything else except the glint from the medal as it swung. When he had finished, Jock stood up and said: 'Happy Birthday,' as he pulled up his jeans.

I lay on the bed, shaking. Down below, I was sore and bleeding. It was the end of my childhood. And it felt like the end of my life. The lines from 'Bright Eyes' about the light that burned so brightly now burning pale swirled through my head, never more apt.

Jock walked out and switched on his music loudly in the next room. Pink Floyd blared from his bedroom and I clamped my hands over my ears, terrified. For the rest of my life I would associate his music with immeasurable pain. I had a shower to try to wash it all off – the blood, the shame, the revulsion. But no matter how much I scrubbed, my skin prickled with it. I could smell him. I could hear his breath, loud in my ears. I could not escape him. And yet I had never felt more alone. That night I found it impossible to concentrate on my *Famous Five* book. I could no longer read stories full of childish make-believe and happy endings. I could no longer be George, chasing pirates and smugglers, drinking ginger beer and eating sandwiches by the sea. That part of me was dead now.

It was late one night, soon afterwards, that I went downstairs in my nightie to get a drink. I had suffered with violent nightmares and anxiety since Jock had raped me and I often woke up, unsettled and scared. A hot drink would usually ease it. Although back then I still didn't even know what it was. I had no label for it.

The rest of the house was asleep, except for my parents, who were both at work: Mum at the pub, Dad at the mine. As I crept into the kitchen, Jock suddenly appeared from the shadows and wrenched me backwards into the living room.

'Quiet,' he hissed.

I screeched in panic before he clamped his hand over my mouth, using his free arm to drag me behind the L-shaped brown and white couch. He pulled down my underwear and my mouth ran dry. I knew what was coming and my whole body screamed out in protest.

'Please, Jock,' I begged, muffled through his fingers. 'Please, no.'

But he was in auto-mode again, eyes staring and glassy. It was as though he couldn't hear or see me. Again the pain was unbearable, again I tried to focus on something else, the stitching down the back of the couch, the St Christopher necklace, the rub of the carpet, rough against my bare legs. But as Jock grunted and sweated, and my heart hammered against my nightie, I heard a noise in the hallway. Definitely, there it was. A door opening.

'Someone's coming,' I gasped, flooded at once with fear and relief.

I expected Jock to stop, to panic and run away, but he didn't seem capable. His expression, driven and fixed, didn't even change. In the next moment Dad was standing above us, at the end of the couch.

'What the bloody hell is going on here?' he shouted.

It was the shock Jock needed and he snapped to his senses, scrambling to his feet and yanking his trousers up. My little hands were trembling as I pulled my knickers up; crimson with shame, as though I was the one at fault.

'Go to bed, Maureen,' said Dad shortly.

I didn't need telling twice. I ran from the room, up the stairs, and threw myself onto my bed, threading the pink bedspread between my fingers, desperate for comfort. I left Jock downstairs to face what I presumed was the harshest of punishments.

That night I cried myself to sleep as always. But this

time they were tears of relief, balm on my poor, weary cheeks. My nightmare was over.

The next morning I was brushing my teeth in the bathroom when my mother came in behind me and cornered me against the sink. To my amazement, she slapped me hard across the face.

'You dirty whore,' she hissed. 'You dirty little bitch.'

I didn't understand. Clutching my smarting cheek, I listened in dismay as she insisted that I must have encouraged Jock in some way. That I was just as much to blame as he was.

'You shouldn't be playing around with your brother like that,' she scathed. 'If I ever catch you two fucking again, you're in serious trouble.'

I couldn't fathom it. I was genuinely and devastatingly stumped. At nine years old I didn't know how to lead a boy on, and certainly not a member of my own family. What had I done wrong? But even then, though I lacked the education and the knowledge to describe my ordeal, I knew instinctively, with every bone in my young body, that what Jock had done was not right. So why was I being blamed?

'I'm sorry,' I whispered limply. 'I'm sorry, Mum.'

'You had better be, my girl,' she said, and she slammed out of the bathroom.

Despite Mum's bizarre reaction, I hoped that this would be the end of the whole horrible affair and I would be left alone. Certainly, Jock didn't come near me and I started to think I could put it behind me. But two weeks on, I woke in the night with a fever and a burning sensation in my throat. The next morning I could hardly swallow.

'Looks like you've got tonsillitis,' Mum said, when I opened my mouth.

'I can't go to school,' I croaked. 'I feel awful.'

I loved school. I would never have chosen to stay at home unless it was absolutely necessary.

'Well, I can't bloody well look after you,' Mum complained. 'I have to go out. And then I've got work.'

But it turned out that Dad was on a late shift, so he and I were left in the house together. I spent the day in bed, and all through the morning I was too poorly even to read, struggling to sip a glass of water. In the afternoon he came into the bedroom and said:

'How're you feeling, Mo-Jo?'

I shrugged and smiled.

'Not too bad, thanks,' I replied. 'A bit better, I think.'

He looked serious, his brow furrowed and his ginger hair uncombed. There was a whiff of Old Spice and sweat about him; it was familiar, comforting. Endearing even. But then he sat on the bed, close enough for me to smell his breath, and suddenly I could see Jock in that same spot, and alarm bells screamed in my head. I lay, frozen with terror, as he began rubbing his hand up and down my leg, each time a little further, a little nearer to my underwear. Up and down. Up and down. It was like watching Jock's necklace swing back and forth, back and forth. Then he pulled down his trousers and forced himself on me, his huge bulk almost suffocating me. The pain was horrific, it felt as though my internal organs were being crushed and pulped. The agony was so all-consuming that I couldn't even scream. It took everything I had just to breathe. Just to survive it. And then, just as I felt I might faint from the trauma, I felt myself floating up from the bed, away from John Wood, and away from the horror. Silently, I handed the suffering to my other self, and watched, half-hypnotised, half-horrified, as he raped me. Then I glided away, even further.

Deep, deep in the recesses of my mind, I was sitting in a tree, reading a *Famous Five* book, with the sun on my face. I could feel the leaves fluttering against my skin. I could smell the sap. I was a little girl again.

Afterwards, he stroked his ginger goatee beard and said: 'Don't worry, I have had the snip.'

That meant nothing to me.

Then he snarled: 'If you tell anyone, I will kill you. Your brothers and sisters will go to a children's home and it will be your fault. Remember that.'

That meant everything to me.

He strode out of the room, slapping his belt closed as he went. He seemed angry. As though this was my fault. Again.

My insides were burning, raw and ripped apart. I stripped the bed, which was covered with blood, and scrubbed my skin in the shower until it was pink and raw. Three days later, my period started. But again, I'd had no sex education and I had no idea what this was. Instead I stared at my knickers in dismay, convinced that something was broken inside me. My body could not have sent me a clearer metaphor.

Each morning, I was desperate to get to school, and especially so now after the rapes. It was the closest I had to a safe space, and I loved learning. I was bright at school, always interested and well-behaved, and I was popular with the teachers and, by now, some of the children, too. One afternoon, as I daydreamed out of the classroom window, I heard sniggering behind me and a hand shot in the air.

'Miss,' said a voice. 'Miss! Maureen Donnelly has got blood all down her leg, Miss.'

I was mortified. I was taken out of the classroom in front of everyone, trying desperately and failing miserably to hide the big blotch of blood on my skirt. My teacher had always been kind and caring towards me, but now, as I walked down the corridor with her, alone, a shiver ran through me. And I wondered whether she was one of *them* as well?

Were all adults evil? Did other parents do unspeakable things to their children behind closed doors, too? I doubted whether I could trust any adult. The rape by John Wood had disturbed me to the point that I saw a malevolence in everyone.

The school nurse called my mum and she came from home to collect me. She shot me a glare and frogmarched me across the playground, and I knew I was in trouble. Yet again. Once we got through the front door, she snapped: 'It's a period, Maureen. Everybody has them. Deal with it.

'Make sure you never go interfering with your brother again. We don't want any babies in this house.'

She tossed a packet of sanitary towels at me and marched out of the room and out of the house.

The following day, I ran away. I didn't plan it. I didn't even expect it. In fact, I took myself by surprise as I walked straight past our house on my way home from school. It wasn't that I wanted to run away – more that I couldn't bring myself to go home. Most kids dreaded going to school, but I dreaded going home. I dreaded walking into the lions' den.

Today, I continued walking, past our gate, down the street, across the main road and to the park. Not the local park, where I knew I'd be easily found; I went to a park on the other side of town. I sat on the swings and read *The Railway Children*, page by page, chapter by chapter, losing myself and forgetting my troubles, in another world. It grew dark but I wasn't in the least bit frightened. Whatever danger lurked in the park, it was nothing to what I faced in my own home. I had been there maybe three hours when a policeman tapped me on the shoulder and said:

'Are you Maureen Donnelly?'

I peered at him, more impressed than frightened.

'How do you know that?' I asked.

'Your parents are very worried about you,' he said gently. 'Come on, let's get you home.'

I had no choice but to go with him, and as we walked to the police car a small part of me was bursting to tell him, desperate to share the horror of my existence. I wanted him to ask the question.

'So how are things at home?'

'So is your stepdad kind to you?'

If only he had asked, then I could have replied. But he said nothing, and so nor did I. We arrived home, and I braced myself. I knew I was safe whilst the police were in the house, but the moment they left I got a good hiding, with Mum punching me all the way up the stairs and into bed.

'That'll teach you,' she growled.

But it didn't, and that was the first time of many. I ran away often – sometimes out of desperation, sometimes out of spite. Sometimes I just wanted to see if anyone would miss me – and quite often they didn't. Anything, anywhere, was better than home. I was fast learning that family was not to be trusted. And home was not a safe place to be.

Chapter 3

I was not close to my siblings. Perhaps that was a failing in me, or maybe there was a lack on both sides, but Mum had made sure of it, too. We had mealtimes in silence. We weren't allowed to talk, to laugh, to bond. She pitted us against each other, punishing one for the other's mistakes. It was row after row after row. If one missed a patch of dust on the coffee table, we'd all get a belt. If one was in trouble at school, we'd all be grounded.

'That'll teach you, you little bastards,' she would yell.

Back then, I didn't understand her motivation for cultivating such animosity between her children. It seemed so calculated and warped. Looking back now, I could maybe assume that she didn't want us to be friends, didn't want us to confide in each other, didn't want us to share secrets. Knowing what lay ahead, perhaps she was simply covering her own back. But the distance was my doing, too. I shrank back and isolated myself, frightened to let anyone in. I was wary of all adults and terrified of all relatives. The more secrets I had to tell, the less I opened my mouth. I was stuck in a downward and perverse cycle.

After the abuse started, I began refusing to change my clothes. I would wear the same underwear for days on end. Perhaps, subconsciously, it was an attempt to make myself as unappealing and unattractive as possible. Or maybe I was slowly, painfully, giving up on myself. I was withdrawing from life. Whatever the reasons, my siblings were understandably disgusted.

'You dirty little tramp,' they taunted. 'Change your clothes, Dozy-Mosey. You smell!'

Far from being upset by the comments, I welcomed them. I liked the fact that I was marked out. Apart. Alone. I didn't want to be part of their family anyway. I was bad-tempered and nasty, caustic even, and I took an obtuse pleasure in knowing that I was getting on their nerves.

'I'm not having a bath and I'm not getting changed, so there,' I replied. 'What exactly are you going to do about it?'

Possibly it was a way of downloading my pain. I was suffering and I wanted them to suffer, too. I had no words for what I was going through, so I diverted my agony through other channels. Or perhaps I just didn't get on with them. It was as simple as that. I was an outsider.

Just before I turned ten I came home from school one day to find a strange man sitting in the living room.

Mum was standing by the fireplace with a face like thunder.

'Well, aren't you going to say hello to your dad?' said the man, standing up to greet me.

I looked at him in confusion.

'My dad is at work,' I said.

His face dropped, and it was only then that I realised he was my biological father. There was an awkward silence and some stilted conversation as I hung around in the doorway, and then he left. And I didn't ever see him again.

To the outside world, John Wood was a good, hardworking man. He had taken on five children to bring up as his own. He kept us in check, held our hands when we were little, made sure we brushed our teeth, went to school, did our homework. He was to be admired and respected. In the local pub he was popular, well-liked. The sort of man nobody had a bad word to say about. The injustice of it was almost too much to bear. Nobody had the slightest idea what he was really like.

Behind the closed doors of our home I was living on my nerves, walking on broken glass, waiting for the next attack. I knew it was coming. I could feel it. And I was powerless to stop it.

Jock vanished from the house one day and we were told by my furious mother that he had 'gone away' after getting into trouble for fighting.

'He won't be back,' she said with a thin smile. 'He'll have to learn to look after himself now.'

Despite everything, I felt a pang of sympathy. I just couldn't help myself; he was my big brother. But my overriding emotion was one of relief. I was safe from him, at least. Yet it was like escaping a rat to then be faced with a poisonous snake. And I had nowhere to hide.

The second rape by John Wood was in my bedroom, like the first. There was only me and him around.

Again, he said to me: 'You can't get pregnant. I've had the snip.'

I stared blankly.

'A vasectomy,' he explained. 'Look it up in one of your bloody books.'

But I had absolutely no idea what he was referring to. I didn't know how babies were made, never mind how to prevent a pregnancy. All I knew was that I was trapped in a nightmare – and it was stuck on repeat. It happened again. And again.

As the weeks went on, I worked out that John Wood would only strike when the house was empty. As long as there were people around, I knew I was safe. But it was a little like waiting for the tide to come in; everything would seem OK, with the water lapping around my toes, then suddenly there were danger signals flashing. A door banged. Someone shouted goodbye. We were alone. And the tide rushed in over my head, and I was drowning, my lungs bursting, my eyes popping.

Every time there was an opportunity, he took it. It could be once a month, or twice a week. The rape was always in my bedroom, and it was always the same routine. It never lasted very long, though it didn't feel that way to me. And sometimes it was rushed and frantic, as if he was anxious about getting caught. He never spoke, except when it was over, to warn me keep me my mouth shut.

'Or else,' he threatened, his pale eyes drilling into mine, his goatee beard scratching against my cheeks. 'Or else, you little bitch.'

And that was that. He was gone, striding downstairs, to wait for my mother to come home. And I was left in bed, doubled over in pain and choking on my own sadness.

Soon after my tenth birthday, late one night, I got up to go to the loo.

Mum had been at work that evening and John Wood had gone along to the pub, after his own shift finished, to wait for her. He filled in as a steward there when he wasn't working down the mine. The front door slammed and woke me as they arrived home late. I heard them getting into bed and, soon after, I decided I needed a quick wee. As I crossed the landing, Mum shouted:

'Is that you, Maureen? Bring us a brew, will you?'

I was sleepy and just wanted to slip back into bed, but I knew better than to refuse. I went downstairs and flicked the kettle on; black coffee for him, black tea for her. When I took the drinks into the bedroom, Mum nodded at the TV and said: 'Come and watch this with us.'

I looked at the small TV at the foot of their bed, where a Hammer House of Horror film was showing.

'Don't want to, I'm tired,' I mumbled.

'You'll do as you're told,' she snapped, her tone suddenly sharp.

Gingerly, I got into the bed, feeling uncomfortable and on edge. Mum was not at all tactile or affectionate, and this just wasn't like her at all. I couldn't remember ever having been in bed with her before. The mixed-up smells of Old Spice aftershave, Charlie perfume and stale, sour booze made my eyes water. I didn't feel safe. And yet I didn't know why.

The horror film was frightening, and instead of looking at the TV I looked around the room at the chest of drawers, the bedside cabinets, the greeny-blue carpet and the yellow flowery curtains. They had a matching quilt, too. Unlike us, they had a duvet – the very latest invention. I remembered feeling envious when they bought it. Now I was under it I couldn't wait to get out. The greeny-blue carpet was spotless, which was no surprise. Part of my rota was to clean their bedroom. But it didn't look the same, not in the dark, not with Mum and him on either side of me.

I must, eventually, have dozed off, despite myself. And when I woke later I had a horrible, scratching feeling down below. Suddenly, horribly, wide awake, I realised there were fingers inside me.

'Please stop,' I begged. 'Please.'

I looked at Mum, pleading with her, hoping she would tell John Wood to stop. But she just smirked and said:

'No. You're enjoying it.'

And I realised, as I took in the scene, that the fingers inside me belonged to my mother. The bile rose up my throat and I recoiled in disgust.

'What are you doing?' I shouted. 'Please stop.'

But neither of them took any notice. John Wood was watching, his long, thin face rapt with concentration, like he was watching a great film.

'You have to do the same to your mum now,' he ordered.

I shook my head and tried to wriggle back from him, but he grabbed my hand forcibly and took two of my fingers, along with two of his. Mum began moaning loudly and the sound made me retch violently.

'I don't want to do this,' I sobbed.

Mum stared at me for a few moments, and then she said to John Wood: 'If you want to have sex with me, you have to do it with her first.'

And so that was what they did. He raped me whilst my own mum watched. I could hear her groaning and murmuring her approval. I bit down on my hand, with my eyes tightly closed, and my other self, floating away across the room, disassociated and divorced from my broken little body. My other self sat down quietly on the chest of drawers, reading a book and swinging her legs, until it was finished.

Once it was over, Mum said: 'Get back in bed and keep your mouth shut.'

I lay awake all night, and the next day, numb with shock, I expected an announcement, a revelation of some sort. But Mum didn't refer to it at all. She stayed in bed late on Sunday morning, as usual, and then chased me out to play with my siblings in the afternoon.

'Back at 5 p.m. for tea,' she told us.

Everything was just as normal. I even questioned whether I was going mad, whether I might have dreamt the whole episode. The weekend came around again, and nothing happened. I tried to tell myself it had been a one-off, as I had with Jock. But somehow I knew that just wasn't true.

Sure enough, two weeks on, Mum crept into my room and shook me roughly by the shoulder.

'Come on,' she whispered loudly. 'Wake up and come with me.'

As I trailed obediently behind her, the tears splashed down my nightie and onto my bare feet. It was just a few steps from my room to theirs. In some ways it felt like the longest walk, as though I was walking to the gallows. But at the same time, it was over too soon. I wanted to walk forever. The scene was surreal. Mum wore her winceyette nightdress and John Wood had his paisley pyjamas on. They looked for all the world like a run-of-the-mill middle-aged couple, in any suburban bedroom. Yet they could not have been more abnormal, more depraved, more inhuman. I longed to escape. I longed to be another little girl, to join a different family, where I was loved and wanted. Not for sex. But just for me.

It became a fortnightly horror. Every other Saturday, Mum and Jock Wood would rape and sexually abuse me in their bed. I was made to endure unimaginable horrors, which, though I tried to block them out, burned through the lining of my soul and ravaged my very core. I hated too that my body reacted to their touch, and I felt like my own body was betraying me. I hated this, so why was my body saying otherwise?

I had no idea why they did it every second Saturday, except perhaps that it fitted in with John Wood's shift patterns. But I dreaded the allotted suffering, the alternate weekends of misery and despair. One of them would steal, like slime, into my room in the middle of the night to wake me. They slithered into my dreams like vile slugs, dragging me out of sleep and into the devils' den. It got to the stage where I would not, could not, sleep on those designated Saturdays. Instead, I waited, wired and anxious, dreading the forthcoming meeting with my nemesis. If there was a purgatory in Stoke-on-Trent it was here, in my bunk bed.

At first I was terrified. I would protest, struggle even, against the wickedness. But as time went on I became resigned. What could I do? One Sunday morning, after a night of abuse, I woke up in such pain that I could barely move.

'I can't take any more,' I thought miserably. 'I can't go on.'

I had no plans to run away, but I found myself at the front door, heading off up the street, without any plan at all of what I was going to do. I didn't take any money, I didn't even take a coat.

And though it hurt to walk, the pain somehow propelled me forwards. I focused on the pain; it almost helped me to keep going. And I was so desperate, I would have walked away on two broken legs if I'd had to.

Later in the day I found myself outside a local school, not my own. I climbed over the perimeter fence and wandered around the playground. I realised I was starving with hunger, but it was not enough to send me back home. And the longer it went on, the harder it got. I imagined my mother's wrath and I could not face it. When darkness came, I managed to loosen a trap door on a coal store and creep inside. It was dark and dingy but warm, because I was up against the boiler, and rather cosy, too. Strangely, I was not at all scared. This was not nearly as frightening as being in my own bed at home. I fell asleep much easier than I'd expected, and the next thing I knew, there was a man's voice invading my dreams.

'She's just a kid,' he was shouting. 'We need to ring the police. She's filthy, covered in coal.'

I scrambled to my feet and he helped me outside. I blinked against the bright light of the morning. It turned out he was the school caretaker and he was about to open up the school for the children to arrive.

'You should be at school yourself,' he said. 'Let's get you home and into a hot bath.'

The police came and they were not so understanding. Clearly they knew I had run away in the past and they had me down as a delinquent and a time-waster.

'You're putting your parents through all this unnecessary pain,' said the policeman harshly. 'Why can't you just behave yourself?'

Dad was at work, but Mum was home when we arrived. She was all smiles with the policemen, but the moment they left she gave me a belt.

'Don't try that stunt again,' she shouted. 'Now get your school uniform on and get out of my sight.'

I was packed off to school with a hollow feeling inside that was about much more than me missing my breakfast.

Two Saturdays on, it was business as usual. I could see no way out. I had tried running away, I had tried to object. If I cried, Mum gave me a slap and told me shut up.

'Nobody likes to listen to a snivelling kid,' she would say.

My only defence against it, as their beery breath bore down on me, was to leave my own body and watch it happen, high above the bed. Detached and separate, I could remain impassive. Untouched. Unhurt.

It got to the stage, if I concentrated very hard, where I could actually physically leave the room whilst I was being raped. I would hover over the bed, before floating down the stairs and into the living room. I could sit for a while at the dining table, or even have a nosy around the kitchen, just to keep my mind focused. I didn't go back to my own body until it was done. And so, in my child's mind, it wasn't happening to me. And yet, in the lonely hours after it was over, I would lie in my own bed and wonder why.

I wondered whether maybe this was how parents showed their love for their children? Or was it because I had done something bad? I was not a particularly attractive child – could this be a form of punishment? Or was it because they loved me the most? Had I done something wrong – or right – to be targeted in this way? I couldn't work it out. It was a warped rationale, but I was so desperate to be loved. I wanted to believe that the abuse stemmed from something good – that I was loved and wanted and cherished. Yet each time my mother laid a finger on me, each time she watched her husband raping me, it was another step into the jaws of hell. Her abuse, more so than any other, destroyed me. It was the ultimate betrayal.

She had carried me, given birth to me, pushed my pram and held my hand. And now, day by day, she was ruining me. This horror laid the foundations for a complex relationship with my mother, which would alternately threaten my sanity and give me hope. She was both the disease and the cure. I hated her and yet I could not help loving her, perhaps in equal measure.

After they had finished with me, I would tiptoe back to bed and, incredibly, over time, I learned to shut it out and I was able to sleep. It was a coping mechanism. A way of keeping my head bobbing above water – but only just. The following morning I would retch with revulsion as I cleaned my teeth, battling to shut out the monstrous scenes that played, constantly, at the periphery of my mind. And the anticipation was almost worse than the event itself.

Every other Saturday morning the panic would build inside me like a furnace, until it was boiling hot. To me, it was monumental. All-consuming. And it floored me that nobody else seemed to even notice. Life carried on around me, just as normal. My sisters would giggle and bicker. We'd eat tea at 5 p.m. Mum would get ready for work. She was always well turned-out and respectable, and so were we. Was that pride in her own appearance and pride in her family? Or was it her way of making sure that nobody asked questions, that nobody suspected that she was a witch in a Marks and Spencer dress? And all the while, the tension bubbled and bubbled.

All evening I would either play in the street or read my books with the anxiety hanging over me like a noose – a noose just big enough for a small girl's neck. And in the bedroom, whilst my sisters played music or read teen magazines, I would stare at my book, sometimes fixed on the same page for hours, as my stomach churned and my brain shuddered.

'What's up with you?' they'd ask. 'You're a bit quiet.'

I couldn't believe that nobody had cottoned on. If there were any near misses, I never knew. Did any of my siblings ever find out? Did no one get up for a wee or a drink on those hideous Saturday nights and wonder why my bed was empty? Were there no relatives or neighbours or teachers who noticed there was something wrong? I wondered again whether maybe it wasn't wrong after all. Whether perhaps this was what all families did and that it was just a part of growing up, a rite of passage. Or, I realised sadly, there was a possibility that people knew what I was going through but they turned a blind eye. They just didn't care.

So, with no other choice, I learned to stay quiet, I learned to accept it. I was a child caught in an adult web of evil. 'Sex with the parents' became an item on the rota, like 'hoovering the bedroom' or 'cleaning the kitchen'. It was as much a part of my routine as dusting the windowsills. Tragically flippant, perhaps, but horribly true. And piled on top of the fortnightly abuse by my parents, I also had Jock to contend with. Though he had now left home, aged fifteen, he would sneak back whenever the rest of the family was out, to rape me.

I'd hear him banging into the house through the back door and shouting up the stairs, to make sure the place was empty. Once he had made sure we were alone, he would strike. He took his chances, whenever he could, grabbing me on Black Bank and dragging me into the bushes, or ambushing me by the pond. He always took me back to that same spot, with the long ferns and the itchy grass. Even if I was playing out with my friends, he was bold enough to yank me out of the group and take me away. And, of course, they never gave it a second thought. Why would they? What would I have to fear from my own big brother?

'Please Jock, no,' I sobbed. 'Please don't.'

Though I pleaded with him to stop, I never tried to run away from him. I was too frightened and too subservient and I knew he'd catch me anyway. My fate would be so much worse if I tried to escape him, I was sure of that. And through it all, Jock never spoke once. I had no idea if he knew that Mum and John Wood were abusing me, or if they knew what he was up to, despite them having warned him to stop. The idea that I had been targeted twice – possibly without obvious connection and collusion – left me desolate. And from that sprung the conviction that this must be my fault.

If I had been targeted by three members of my own family, then surely I was to blame? Evidently, I had done something to trigger this. But what? I felt dehumanised and brutalised. I was nothing more than a scrap of meat to my own family. And yet still, I longed to be loved.

Chapter 4

A few months after the regular abuse began, I began suffering from persistent urine infections. I was in a lot of pain at home, which didn't seem to bother Mum much, but it was affecting my schoolwork, too, because I was forever asking to go to the toilet in class. Mum didn't like the teachers asking any questions at all. She didn't like any attention on our family, so she made an appointment with the GP. But, of course, she made me suffer for it.

'You're nothing but trouble,' she snapped.

I was back and forth from the doctors for a few weeks, and when several courses of antibiotics made no difference I was referred to a urologist at the hospital. Mum was at work when the appointment came around, so John Wood took me instead. I felt so anxious, being on my own with him. I had visions of him raping me at some point during the appointment. I knew there were beds at the hospital – would he lock me in a room and do it there? I wasn't sure what was and wasn't socially acceptable any more. I shrank back, like a frightened animal, every time his hand brushed mine on the bus journey there.

'We'll need a urine sample from you,' the nurse said, when we arrived.

I had no idea how to pee into the small sample bottle I was given and I looked questioningly at John Wood after she had gone. I didn't want to even speak to him, but there was nobody else.

'For God's sake,' he growled. 'Just piss into the bottle. It's not difficult.'

'I'll do my best,' I nodded. 'I promise.'

But whether it was the infections or my nerves, I just couldn't do it. I sat in the toilet, with tears running down my face, wondering how on earth I was going to get out of yet another mess. In the end, John Wood marched into the ladies' toilets with a paper cup and demanded I use that instead. The idea of him in the girls' toilets, invading my space yet again, left me trembling. Would he attack me here – in the cubicle? I just didn't know.

When at last I produced a sample, we went in to see the specialist.

'Can you think of a reason why Maureen might be getting so many infections?' asked the doctor. 'Is there any chance she could be sexually active at her young age?'

John Wood shook his head.

'You do understand what I'm saying to you?' the doctor pressed.

This time John Wood nodded.

'I'm absolutely sure,' he replied.

I didn't know exactly what they were talking about, but I was slowly working out that what happened to me at weekends had some connection with 'sexual activity'. And I wondered whether perhaps this doctor might step in and put a stop to it. It was a faint glimmer of hope and I clung to it. But when the next assigned Saturday night came around, and I was abruptly awoken during the night, I realised I had been foolish to count on the medical profession.

One afternoon soon after, as I played outside with some pals, we came across an old bike in the street without a seat. It was rusty and probably destined for the tip, but it gave us something to do. We all tried to ride it, and when I jumped on, the springs pinched me and cut into my groin.

The following day I was in pain, and again, I struggled to go to the toilet.

'I can't have a wee,' I told Mum. 'There's something wrong.'

Grumbling, she made an appointment with the GP, who sent us straight to hospital. There I was examined by another doctor, who frowned and said to Mum: 'Do you realise your daughter is no longer a virgin? She's only ten years old.'

Mum shook her head irately.

A Family Secret

'She sat on a bike pole, that's all there is to it,' she retorted.

I felt another flicker of hope that perhaps now something would be done. Alarm bells would ring. Surely this doctor would ask me some questions and get some help? But instead, I was sent home with some antibiotic cream and that was the end of it. Except, of course, Mum gave me a clip around the back of the head for bringing trouble to the family.

As with our clothes, she was always careful to make sure we wore good school shoes and we had the correct uniform. We had regular haircuts, and we saw dentists and doctors when necessary. Looking back now, I feel it had nothing to do with maternal instincts and it was all about keeping up appearances.

Each weekend, too, she and John Wood would take two of us to the pub for a few drinks, and it was the highlight of our month. I loved going with them, but I was rarely chosen.

'You never behave yourself, Mo-Jo,' Mum would tell me, her lip curling. 'You need to be a good girl.'

There was a kids' room at the pub, with games and a snooker table, and it was usually full of children from our estate. At the time I thought it was a treat, a genuine effort on Mum's part to be nice. Now again, I wonder whether she was just playing a game, glossing over the grim depravity of our home life with a veneer of respectability. It was all about how she was thought of and not what she was actually like.

Aside from the sexual abuse, she was physically and mentally cruel, too. I can't remember her taking me on outings much, or on any proper holidays. Once, all seven of us piled into a Reliant Robin and drove all the way to Glasgow to see our grandparents. We got a puncture near Loch Lomond and had to wait by the roadside whilst she and John Wood argued about fixing it. But I loved that trip, every minute of it. I was surrounded by relatives the whole time, so I knew I was safe from wandering hands and mouths. Up there, I felt like my soul was washed out and clean again. But as soon as we were back home, it started again. And I retreated, like a frightened animal, back into my shell.

Our local working men's club organised an annual trip to the Blackpool seaside, which was always an eagerly awaited event. It felt like our whole estate emptied out for the day. When we arrived, Mum would usually dump us in the Fun House and go to the pub. But it was a day out and it was such fun.

Many years later I would read about child sex exploitation in Blackpool and smile bitterly at the irony. Even on a day out, I never really escaped it. The summer after the abuse started, Mum didn't allow me to go.

'You've been naughty,' she said. 'You can stay at home. On your own.'

Maybe she didn't want me spending time with other adults in case I spilled the beans. Maybe she just hated me. Either way, there was no point in arguing. I bit back tears as the coach pulled away from the club car park.

But in truth, having the house to myself for the whole day turned out to be absolutely glorious. It was hot and sunny in Stoke, and I sneaked out to play and to buy sweets, even though I had been forbidden to leave my bedroom. In the afternoon I spent hour after peaceful hour reading my book, and I wished and wished they would never come back. When the coach returned I was thrilled to hear that the trip had been a disaster and it had rained all day.

'We couldn't get near the promenade,' Mum complained. 'The weather was dreadful.'

I couldn't help thinking it was just what they deserved and maybe, just maybe, there was someone on my side after all.

I had always enjoyed learning, but after the abuse began school became my refuge. Even if I was ill, or out of sorts, I was up and dressed in my uniform way before the alarm clock every morning. I literally couldn't wait to leave the house. The place was suffocating. It pushed down on me like a physical weight, threatening, at times, to crush me completely. I was constantly on edge, always afraid, always anxious of what would happen next. It was all the more frightening because I couldn't work out what I had done to deserve such brutality. I still suspected, in fact I was becoming increasingly convinced, that it was all my own fault. But I knew I had no chance of curing the problem unless I could identify what it was.

In the sanctuary of my school I was a different child. I was bright and alert. I did my homework, and more besides. I read more than ever before, too, but now my children's books held no appeal. Since the abuse started I'd found the *Famous Five* and the *Secret Seven* totally unpalatable. It wasn't so much that I had outgrown my old favourites, more that I had been wrenched out of that world and flung into another. Instead, I moved on to reading J. R. R. Tolkien, Jane Austen, Thomas Hardy and F. Scott Fitzgerald. I drank in the tragedies and the heartbreak and the raw injustice of life. This was my world now.

With my head in the pages of *The Lord of the Rings*, I could, at last, lose myself. I could forget who I was and what was happening to me. The two sides of Sméagol were like the two sides of myself. He battled against what he didn't want to hear. I fought against what I didn't want to feel. I felt a pathetic empathy with the creature. I knew how it felt to be tortured. And to be an outsider.

I struggled still with friendships. I had never had many schoolfriends, but now the few I had seemed so dreadfully silly and immature. I no longer wanted to skip or giggle with other ten-year-olds. I certainly didn't want to play dolls, mummies and daddies, happy families. I was a world-weary adult in a child's body, bitten by life.

One afternoon, after school, there was a knock at the door and I heard strange voices in the hallway. I was reading in my bedroom but I peered over the bannister to listen in.

'A report about your children ... Mrs Wood ... we take this seriously ...'

Mum nodded and agreed and put on her best posh voice as she ushered them out of the house.

'I completely agree,' she was saying. 'It's a malicious report. Absolutely unfounded.'

She waited until their car was out of sight, then she flung open the front door, stuck her chin out into the street, and yelled, to nobody in particular: 'If I find out which one of you bastards it was, you're dead.'

I hadn't a clue what was going on but I ran back into my bedroom quickly, before she turned her temper on me. Years later, many years later, it would all become clear.

Aged eleven, I moved, with my friends, to St John Fisher RC High School. It was a big event for us all, and to me the school seemed enormous. But by now I was settling down into a group of girls, and although I was considered the quiet one and, quite possibly, the weird one, I did at least have a sense of belonging. As they hit puberty, the only topic of conversation was boys.

'I fancy him, do you fancy him, Maureen? Do you want me to ask him out for you? Would you snog him?'

Their chatter both bored me and confused me. I stared ahead, blankly, unable even to pretend to join in. They wore makeup and bought tighter tops and shorter skirts.

But I dreaded the idea of attracting a boy. The thought of kissing someone was repulsive. I refused to wear makeup. I dressed in baggy clothes and tracksuits, making myself as unappealing and unremarkable as I could.

'We can't work you out, Maureen,' my friends laughed. 'You're such a funny girl.'

Our education broadened out, too, and we began studying Biology, and with it sexual education. Ours was a Roman Catholic school so it was hardly explicit, but as I listened to the explanations of how sexual intercourse was performed – 'between two loving people, a husband and a wife' – I had a sudden and sickening awakening. This was it. This was exactly what my own parents had been doing to me.

The lessons went on. We had to label male and female genitalia. We had to learn about the different stages of conception. The kids around me collapsed into helpless giggles as they wrote 'cervix' and 'penis' on their worksheets. But I sat in silence, cold with the realisation that I was being sexually abused.

'It's not funny!' I wanted to shout. 'It's disgusting! You should avoid it for as long as you can!'

But nobody noticed my shaking hands and my blanched face. Our teacher was a stunted man who was probably more embarrassed than most of the students. He was not someone I could confide in. And my friends, though they meant well, could never have understood. Theirs was a world so far removed from mine, it might as well have been in a different galaxy. There was one

girl in our class who wore the latest clothes and trow-
elled on makeup. She was very pretty and all the boys
fancied her. The rest of the girls all envied her and
wanted to be like her. But I felt nothing but pity for her.

'It's not all it's cracked up to be,' I wanted to tell them.
'Trust me, I should know.'

There was one teacher, who was in charge of RE, who
I felt I could talk to. One day I'd had a bust-up with a
friend in the playground and she had helped to sort it
out. She was compassionate and understanding, and I
would often invent scenarios in my head where I blurted
out the truth to her. But every time, despite my rehears-
als, I lost courage at the last minute. The context did not
help; it was a strict Catholic school in the early 1980s
and sex, and sexual abuse, simply was not discussed. It
was kept behind closed doors. In bed. In secret. And
even if it had been less stifling, I still don't think I would
have found the words. I could not share it. It would have
to be coaxed out of me, pulled out of me, like one of the
strands on my pink bedspread.

One day we were in the playground at lunchtime
when Jock roared up to the gates on his motorbike.

'You're wanted at home, Maureen,' he said. 'Mum's
not well.'

I hesitated.

'I'm at school,' I protested. 'I'll get into trouble if I
just walk out.'

Jock wrapped his gloves tighter around the
handlebars.

'I just said, Mum's ill. Now get on the bike.'

I knew better than to argue. I waited until the dinner lady had turned her back and then I slipped out of the gate. Jock handed me a spare helmet and I climbed onto the back of his bike. I knew my friends were watching and probably in awe. But I felt nothing but revulsion. The proximity of him was repugnant. I had no choice but to cling to him as he set off, but I hated touching his waist.

We tore down our street – but went straight past the house – and suddenly, my heart was in my shoes.

'Please, Jock, no,' I begged. 'Let me go back to school.'

But my voice was drowned out in the wind. He pulled up at the bottom of Black Bank and dragged me up there. Amongst the ferns, and in my school uniform, he raped me, without a word.

Then he handed me my helmet and drove me back to school. He left me at the gates and simply disappeared. I sat in class that afternoon, mute with despair. I couldn't concentrate on lessons. I could barely remember my own name.

'You seem to prefer gazing out of the window rather than following the text,' said my history teacher. 'Would you like to share your thoughts with us, Maureen?'

I shook my head numbly. I really would not have known where to start.

Chapter 5

The cycle of abuse and misery continued for three years. Mum and John Wood were as regular and as sickening as clockwork. It was almost as though they had it written in a diary. Jock would visit sporadically and unexpectedly and snatch what he could, when he could. I would watch his St Christopher necklace swinging above my head, back and forth, back and forth, and silently plead for an end to it all.

But compared to the horrors I went through on a Saturday night, the abuse from Jock almost paled into palatability. His attacks were hesitant and fumbling, almost as if he was reluctant. It felt as though he was going through the motions, doing what he was driven to do, for whatever reason. John Wood was a completely different ordeal.

Nothing – but nothing – was more painful or more appalling than the brutal and unforgiving rapes by my stepfather, with my malevolent mother watching on;

a twisted sidekick in a hairnet and a winceyette nightdress.

'Go on, John, go on. She loves it,' she would say.

Her short dark hair was plastered to the sides of her head with sweat. Her eyes were like bullet holes in the darkness. I could feel her long nails scraping at me. I could smell her cheap Charlie perfume and her rancid breath.

'Stop it, stop it. I hate it,' I would plead.

It was early in the spring of 1984, when, aged thirteen, I started feeling sick, mostly in the mornings. I couldn't even turn over in bed without a wave of nausea sloshing over me. The smell of coffee was enough to turn my stomach and I'd baulk if anyone came near me with a cigarette. I noticed changes in my body, too. I had always been stick-thin, like a little match girl. But now I was developing curves and contours. At first I presumed it was puberty, but when my stomach began to curve also, I knew exactly what this was.

We'd finished the sex education classes at school, and I knew how babies were made. But I also knew better than to breathe a word of it.

'Your secret is safe with me, angel,' I whispered, with one hand on my tummy.

I carried the knowledge around with me, like a precious gold pendant, hidden under my clothes. A glorious secret that nobody else knew. I felt like I was carrying a smile with me.

'Nobody knows,' I repeated conspiratorially. 'Just you and me.'

A Family Secret

A couple of weeks later, Mum collared me on the stairs, frogmarched me into her bedroom, and closed the door.

'Are you pregnant?' she demanded.

Just hearing the word out loud sent a frightening thrill through me. I wanted to say it myself too, just to hear it. I wanted it to be true. But I knew I had to be careful.

'No,' I lied. 'Definitely not.'

She pursed her lips and glared at me.

'You'd better bloody not be,' she said menacingly, shoving me back out onto the landing.

Instinctively, I knew she wouldn't let me keep the baby, and already I loved him dearly. This baby, this little heartbeat inside me, felt like the answer to all of my dreams and my hopes. For as long as I could remember, I had wanted to love someone, and for them to love me back. All I wanted was a pure and innocent love. And this was my chance.

'I know you love me,' I whispered, as I stroked my swollen belly. 'And I love you too.'

I told nobody. Instead, I began saving money secretly. I formulated a plan, in the darkness of my bunk bed, to buy a train ticket and to run away to London, where I could raise my baby in peace and anonymity.

'Just me and you,' I told my bump.

It was of course a childish plan and doomed to fail. But then, I was just a child myself.

I kept myself busy, doing odd jobs for the neighbours, tidying gardens, running errands and doing shopping. I washed cars, too. As soon as my household chores were finished, I'd be out in the street, touting for work.

'Can't play out,' I told my friends. 'I've got stuff to do.'

I had responsibilities, demands and stresses. And I loved it. Little by little, my stash of contraband cash grew. A month later, I counted out the grand total of £30 and my eyes shone as I thought of the possibilities ahead. I hid it behind my chest of drawers, until the time was right.

To keep up pretences, I began wearing baggy clothes – old sweatshirts and tracksuit pants. I had always dressed boyishly anyway, I had never been a girly-girl like my sisters, so I hoped I wouldn't attract too much attention. And, of course, it wasn't as though anyone paid me any attention in the first place. At four months I felt the first stirrings of movement and with them the beginnings of something I had never felt before – pure and unconditional love.

One afternoon, after I'd been cleaning, Mum came into the bedroom to inspect my work. She ran her fingers across the furniture to check for dust and then pulled out the chest of drawers, to make sure I'd hoovered behind it. My heart sank as the little bag of money dropped from its hiding place and onto the carpet.

'What's this for?' she demanded, tipping it out onto the bed. 'Where the hell did you get this?'

'I earned it,' I said truthfully. 'I earned every penny. I'm saving up for something nice.'

Mum scoffed and scooped the lot into her own pocket. My mouth fell open, but there was nothing I could do.

'Girls your age don't need money,' she said. 'You're getting above yourself, Mo-Jo.'

And that was that. I couldn't argue. Now I would have to start again, from scratch, and be so much more careful this time, too.

One Saturday night soon after, when I was around five months pregnant, Mum ordered me into her bedroom for the usual ritual of torture. I could never get used to it, but I was accepting of it. I had to be.

I gripped the sheets, closed my eyes tight and, in my mind's eye, I slipped off the bed away from them. It was with such ease, I could almost have been made of liquid. Noiselessly, gracefully, I glided across the room and settled on the windowsill, away from the slithering hands, away from the stale, stinking breath.

Mum had her fingers inside me, moaning horribly, when suddenly her face froze.

'You lied to me!' she screamed. 'You dirty little bitch!'

In that moment I was sucked back across the room, as if by a vortex, and dumped back into my own body.

'What's going on? What's happening?' John Wood demanded.

'She's fucking pregnant, that's what's going on,' Mum screamed demonically. 'I felt the baby moving inside her. She's a liar.'

John Wood's face was a picture. He looked terrified – truly terrified – for the first time ever. I had never seen him so scared. I scrambled off the bed in alarm, my legs twisting in the quilt, tripping over my own feet as I ran. I closed the door behind me and got into bed, figuring they were less likely to burst in and batter me with my sister sleeping in here too. Under the covers I tried to slow my breathing, with one hand on my belly.

'Don't worry, darling,' I whispered. 'It's going to be fine.'

My fears now were not for me, but for my baby. My heart was hammering against my ribs and I tried desperately to calm down, so that he was not distressed. I waited a while, listening to Mum and John Wood arguing in the bedroom, but they didn't come for me. As I drifted off to sleep I remembered my mother, spittle flying, screaming: 'Dirty little bitch.'

She was the one sexually abusing her own daughter. Yet I was the dirty one.

On Monday morning Mum took me to see the doctor. I could see she was rattled. Really rattled. And although I was fearful, a small part of me was pleased, too. I was glad she was suffering a little because it was long overdue. All the way there she kept up a tirade like a machine gun, spitting out streams of words like bullets.

'We need to get this story straight. You don't know who it was. You were raped by a stranger on your way home one night. A stranger. Got it?

'What happens in our house stays in our house. Remember?

'Don't say a word or you're for it. Mark my words, you are for it.'

I didn't say a thing. It hadn't occurred to me that people would ask who the father was, that people in authority might want to know where my baby had come from.

In any case, I nodded along with Mum. I had no choice.

I found myself sitting in front of a middle-aged doctor, with Mum next to me, a warning finger in the small of my back, in case I even thought about speaking out of line.

'We think she might be pregnant,' Mum said.

The doctor kept a calm expression but checked my notes and said: 'She is only thirteen years old.'

'I know,' Mum nodded, shooting a glare of disapproval at me.

'Oh, I know. It's disgusting, isn't it? She reckons she's been raped. Some stranger, apparently. We want an abortion, don't we? Don't we, Maureen?'

I felt a prod in my back but didn't speak. I didn't even nod. There was no way I was playing this game. Now I had my baby to think of. And though I could never have stood up to Mum for my own sake, I found it remarkably easy to do so for my baby.

I lay on the couch whilst the doctor examined my bump and confirmed what I already knew. He said I was about twenty-two weeks pregnant.

'Your choices will be limited,' he warned. 'I'm sending you to the hospital, right away, for an urgent scan.

She's very young so we need to keep a close eye on things.'

'And what about an abortion?' Mum pressed.

'Let's see what the scan says,' said the doctor briskly.

At the hospital it was pretty much the same procedure. Mum did all the talking and I sat, fizzing with panic at the thought of a termination, brimming with excitement at the thought of seeing my baby on a scan. The waiting room was full of what, to me, seemed like old women. There were pregnant women there old enough to be my grandmother. When my turn came and I stood up, showing off my rounded bump, there were raised eyebrows and tuts. Mum followed behind me, muttering abuse aimed not at them, but at me.

'This gel will feel a bit cold,' smiled the sonographer, as she rubbed my tummy.

The monitor was turned away from me so I couldn't see the baby after all, which was a disappointment. But I broke into a huge smile as I heard the thud, thud, thud of his little heart, echoing out of the machine.

He was real, after all! I hadn't doubted it, but to hear his heartbeat, to know that he was in there, cooking slowly, was joyous.

'Hello, darling,' I whispered silently. 'I won't let anyone hurt you. Don't worry.'

The scan confirmed that I was indeed twenty-two weeks pregnant. I had no idea of the abortion laws and I could only hope that we were too late. As we walked out into the waiting room, we were met by a social worker, alerted, most probably, by my GP.

'We're dealing with this as a family,' Mum said stiffly. 'We don't need any help, thank you.'

I expected that to be that.

But the social worker replied: 'That isn't your decision, Mrs Wood.'

I looked on in interest. Nobody ever stood up to my mother. When she shouted, the neighbours tended to shut their windows. We all jumped to attention and did just as she said. But not the social worker; she seemed happy to go toe to toe with my mother. This was a revelation.

'Your daughter is a child herself. She is the priority,' continued the social worker.

Despite myself, I swelled with pride. I had never been anyone's priority before. I felt really quite important. I was as impressed as Mum was indignant.

'Are we too late for a termination?' Mum snapped.

The social worker nodded.

'She's far too late,' she confirmed. 'So your daughter needs our support, all of our support. We'll be in touch, Mrs Wood.'

Relief flooded through me. I knew we had more challenges ahead, I wasn't stupid enough to think it was over. But I knew my baby was safe, for now at least.

Seething, Mum dragged me outside and kicked me all the way home. It was as if she was trying to kick the baby out of me herself. But I dodged most of her efforts and ignored her ranting.

Maureen Wood

'You're a disgrace. You've brought shame on this family. Your father's at work. Wait till he hears about this. Just you wait.'

We reached our front door and my backside was stinging. And inwardly I was railing against the injustice. She had abused me, and my brother and stepfather had raped me. Yet I was the disgrace. I was the one who had brought our family to its knees.

'It will have to be adopted,' Mum announced. 'There's no way you're keeping it.'

She and John Wood were waiting for me as I came down the stairs the next day. One hand went to my stomach, the other was clamped over my mouth.

'Please,' I breathed. 'Please let me keep my baby.'

But Mum waved me aside angrily. I wasn't even permitted to have a point of view. It was my baby, my body, yet I didn't matter. Nothing had changed.

'You're going up to Scotland tomorrow,' Mum said. 'Get packed and make sure you're ready. It's an early train.'

'Why?' I asked, but Mum's lip curled and I knew I was pushing her too far.

That night, with my overnight bag waiting by my bed, I barely slept. And when I finally managed to doze, I dreamed that I was pushing my baby along a London street, snuggled and safe in a cosy pram. But then coming towards me, her gimlet eyes blazing, was my mother. She poked her long nails into the pram and, as she leaned over, I caught a whiff of her Charlie perfume.

'Where is it? Where's the baby?' she demanded. 'You can't keep it.'

I was panic-stricken, looking around me wildly, praying that help would come. But then Mum began to cackle, her head thrown back, her thick white throat exposed.

'There is no baby, you stupid little bitch,' she sneered. 'You must have left it somewhere.'

And she was right. The pram was achingly empty.

'What have you done with my baby?' I sobbed. 'It was mine. You had no right.'

But Mum was doubled over laughing; so loudly, it gave me a ringing in my ears. And then the alarm clock was bleeping and it was time to get up and catch the train to Glasgow.

The journey was miserable. Mum sat in the seat opposite and glowered at me as though I was nothing more to her than an inconvenience. And if I had hoped for any compassion from my Scottish relatives, I was sadly mistaken.

'How could you do this to your parents?' snarled my aunt, when we arrived. 'You are a disgrace, my girl.'

No doubt she had been fed the same story about me being raped by a stranger, but she did not mention it or question it.

I gathered, from eavesdropping, that she knew a childless couple and that they would be willing to adopt my baby. My mother wanted the whole affair done privately, so that nobody found out. My trip to Scotland was so that I could meet the adoptive couple, presumably so that they could vet me in some way. It certainly wasn't for my benefit. The blood thudded in my ears as I pieced together their plan. How on earth would I get through this?

'Don't worry, angel, I'll think of something,' I said automatically, but without any real conviction.

I was determined not to let my baby go. The idea of handing over a part of myself to complete strangers was abhorrent. I wanted this baby. I knew I couldn't give up my child. I reassured my baby, constantly, that I would keep him with me. That nothing, and nobody, would ever separate us.

'I promise, I promise,' I said quietly.

But though I repeated platitudes, for the baby's sake, deep down, I was panic-stricken. I didn't know how I was going to get out of this mess. The next day, Mum took me across the whole city, to different social services offices, to try to arrange the adoption. But we got the same answer everywhere we went.

'You can't arrange a private adoption,' said the social workers. 'It isn't legal. This has to be done through the proper channels. If you want to place a baby for adoption there are rules you must follow. And we'd need to speak to your daughter first, above all else.'

And no matter how much Mum argued, they wouldn't budge. She frogmarched me back to my aunt's house and

I could barely keep the smile off my face. It was a tiny victory, but a victory all the same, and I felt quietly thrilled. This was another hurdle overcome. Mum furiously packed her case and announced she was returning home – alone.

'What about me?' I asked. 'What's going to happen now?'

But she didn't reply. She stalked out of the house and up the street with her bags, and I watched from an upstairs window. I saw her shoulders sag with relief as she walked away. And it hit me that she was glad to be rid of me. I was a problem to be solved. An embarrassment to be hidden away.

Two long, lonely weeks passed and there was no word from Mum. She had simply washed her hands of me completely.

'So what should I do now?' I asked.

But nobody seemed to know. Then my maternal grandmother took charge. She was a lovely woman and I could never reconcile that she was my mum's mother. They seemed to be such completely different characters. Granny Kelly wrapped her arms around me, smiled, and said: 'You have done nothing wrong, my darling. It will all be OK. Remember how much I love you.'

Her words were so warm. Such a comfort. She was the only person who had shown me any kindness at all since my pregnancy was confirmed. But she also rang my mother and ordered her to face up to her responsibilities and take me home.

'The girl needs her family,' she told my mother sternly. 'Stop ignoring the problem.'

Before I knew it I was on a train, back to Stoke-on-Trent.

In the days that followed, it would become so hard to remember that Granny Kelly loved me. Because it felt like nobody loved me at all.

When I got home I readjusted quickly to the routine, and when Saturday night came around I was on tenterhooks. I didn't see why the abuse would stop just because I was having a baby. Why would they care? But Saturday night came and went, and nothing happened. I braced myself for the following Saturday, but again I got through the night undisturbed. And just as inexplicably as it had started, the fortnightly cycle of abuse came to an end. It was never spoken about or referred to in any way. It simply stopped. And I was eternally grateful. Such was my mentality that I was grateful when I was not being raped.

I never felt completely safe; there was always a worry, especially when I was in bed, that I might be plucked out and savaged. But as time went on that threat diminished, and for the first time in my life I began to look to the future.

My pregnancy seemed to be absolutely textbook. It went like a dream. I had been so skinny before that my bump was very much accentuated. As the weeks passed, I looked comically rounded and I felt like a beached whale. But I loved it. I wasn't tired or hormonal. My ankles didn't swell, I didn't get stretch marks or swollen ankles. I just seemed to bloom. And I chatted away to my baby every day, as though he was already in my arms.

'And after my bath we'll have a little walk,' I told him. 'Fresh air will be good for us both.'

I was no longer alone. I had a best friend – better than that, a soulmate.

Every two weeks I was sent for a scan, to check the baby's growth. And at thirty weeks, when I arrived for my usual check-up, I noticed that the monitor was turned facing towards me. I felt a thrill of anticipation. I was about to see my baby for the very first time. His image flashed up, his short arms and legs, and his fluttery fingers and toes, and every bone in my body melted. And I knew in that moment that I would do everything I could to protect him. I would die for him if I had to.

'My little angel,' I whispered. 'I love you so much.'

I had no idea how I was going to stop the adoption. But I knew that if I had to run away from the hospital, in the dead of night, I would do it. If I had to sleep on the streets, with my baby held close, I would do it. I was prepared to go to any lengths at all to keep him.

'No matter what it takes,' I told myself.

Mum was hostile from the moment I got back from Scotland, but then I was well used to that. The lack of human warmth from my family didn't bother me too much at all, especially when I had such warmth and comfort in my belly.

That September I wasn't allowed to go back to school, and instead social services arranged a home tutor for a couple of hours a week. When she arrived, my first thought was that she looked just like Mary Poppins. Her clothes were rather formal and matronly, but she had a kind twinkle in her eye. I had tuition every Monday, Wednesday and Friday, working away at the pine dining table, painfully aware of Mum tutting loudly every time she walked past me.

'You'd be at school if you hadn't got yourself knocked up,' she would say. 'You dirty little cow.'

Life was very lonely. I wasn't allowed to see my school friends, and I missed them more than I would have thought. I didn't see any of the kids on the street either. I no longer fancied playing manhunt or swimming in the pond. Things had gone past that. Mum would send me to the shop for cigarettes when she ran out, but she rarely spoke to me. I felt like I was ostracised, like she was trying to strip away my identity.

Did I exist – or not?

Occasionally she'd erupt into an outburst and I had no choice but to listen quietly.

'We'll never live this down,' she snapped. 'You've ruined the whole family.'

The police came to interview me, because the story Mum had concocted was that I had been raped on my way home from a school disco.

'Stick to the story,' she warned me. 'Or else.'

I was terrified enough and smart enough to do as she

said. And I didn't find telling lies as hard as I'd expected, because of course I had been raped. The circumstances were different, but the crux of the story was essentially true. I kept the details vague, mumbling something about a man attacking me in a field on my way home in the dark.

Looking back, I feel sure they must have seen through my story. They must have had their suspicions. I was a young girl, with a baby inside me, and I was unable to give them any specifics about the attack. Surely alarm bells were ringing?

'I'm sorry,' I muttered. 'I just can't remember too well.'

There was certainly no investigation, no public appeal, no widespread search. I think the police probably had a good idea of what was going on at home, but without evidence they couldn't do anything.

'Are you sure it was a stranger who attacked you on the field?' asked one policewoman.

I nodded firmly. Years of indoctrination, of living in fear, of being made to believe that I was worthless, were coming to fruition. My mother had done her job well. Yet deep down a part of me was crying out for help. If only the police officer had asked the right question. If only she had asked if anyone at home had ever attacked me too. I wanted to tell her. Yet I could not find a way to tell her myself, without a prompt. If she had drawn it out of me, I could have passed the blame onto the police. It would have been their fault, not mine, when my family fell to pieces.

I had to be examined by a police doctor, too. I was taken to a specialist unit, so sterile and clinically clean it felt sinister to a young teenager like me. I worried that the examination might somehow throw into sharp relief my lies about my attacker. As if perhaps the police doctor might smell the Old Spice and the Charlie perfume and work out what had really been happening to me.

The examination was in fact more traumatic than I had expected. To me, it felt like another episode of abuse; less invasive, more clinical, but another violation all the same. Mum was in the room, holding my hand like the devoted parent, making sure I didn't stray from the script. A slight trace of a smirk played around her lips as the swabs were taken. She was a beast, a fiend hiding behind her sensible sandals and her floral blouse. A monster disguised as a mother.

She thanked the police doctor and made sympathetic little murmurs as they discussed my predicament. She helped me to get dressed again and put a warning hand, disguised as protection, on my shoulder as she steered me outside.

'You remember what I said about keeping your gob shut,' she hissed, as we walked back to the bus stop. 'One word out of you, young lady, and you're in for a good kicking.'

Deep down I felt almost certain that Jock was the baby's father. John Wood had drummed it into me that he couldn't get me pregnant, and I suppose, because I wanted to, that I believed him. But it wasn't just that he'd had a vasectomy; I felt instinctively that the baby was Jock's. It was nothing to do with dates of my periods or the rapes; it didn't even occur to me to work those out. It was just a feeling I had; visceral and intuitive.

I had no idea if Mum even knew that Jock had raped me, and whether she presumed that John Wood was the only suspect in the frame. And in our family there was no communication and no truth. Ours was a tangled and sordid web, with layer after layer of lies and deceit.

John Wood kept his distance whilst I was pregnant. He could hardly bear to be in the same room as me; if I walked in, he would walk straight out again. He didn't make eye contact and never spoke to me at all. Sometimes I would catch him sneaking a look at me, his face creased in worry. And I knew his concern was all for himself, not for me. Possibly he was worried his vasectomy had failed after all, and this was going to come back on him. The due date I had been given was 27 October 1984 – John Wood's forty-first birthday. Did he see that as a sign – a clue from the womb? Or maybe his concern was that I might spill the beans about his abuse to a social worker or a midwife. I had access to so many childcare professionals now, so many people in positions of authority. Perhaps he wished I simply did not exist. It might have been his baby. It might not. Neither of us could know for sure.

Chapter 6

On 5 October 1984 I woke in the early hours with crippling stomach cramps and a dull ache in my lower back. I imagined, with a flush of excitement, these were the first stages of labour. For a while I lay still, simply savouring the knowledge that each cramp, each twinge, was a step closer to me becoming a mummy. Then, as they grew more intense, I got more anxious and I crept into the bathroom and leaned against the sink, groaning. I heard a noise on the landing and realised Mum was awake too. I was worried she might give me a good hiding for disturbing her sleep, but she huffed and puffed, then went across the street to call an ambulance from the neighbour's phone.

I was loaded into the ambulance with my overnight bag and I felt a rush of happiness. This was it. It was finally happening. We went off to hospital, but after a cursory examination by the midwife I was sent back home again.

'It's too early yet,' the midwife told me. 'Come back when the contractions are more regular.'

Mum was unimpressed, but she slept in my bedroom that night, to keep an eye on me. It wasn't lost on me that the last time we'd slept in the same room she had sexually assaulted me, time after time. But now I had to shut it out. I had to focus on my baby.

I dozed off, but at 3 a.m. I woke again, and went downstairs for a hot drink to ease my stomach pain. This time I managed my contractions by myself, breathing deeply, all alone in the living room, watching the first lights of a cold dawn streaking through a grey sky.

'Not long now, angel,' I whispered, cupping my bump with my hands.

Mum woke after 8 a.m. and came marching downstairs to find me.

'Why didn't you wake me?' she demanded.

'I didn't need you,' I replied. 'I was fine.'

But though I was loath to admit it, as the contractions got worse I did need her. I needed her desperately. They tore through my body, strong enough to whip my breath away and leave me shuddering in pain. I was suddenly terrified of the labour, of the pain that lay ahead. I hadn't expected it to be this brutal and now I didn't know what to expect. Part of me thought that if I ignored the whole thing it might not happen. It was a child's approach to an inescapably adult situation. I wanted the baby, but not the labour.

By now the contractions were fierce and regular, and

Mum went over to the neighbour and called another ambulance. But the hospital refused to send a second one, which sent Mum into a rage.

'What do they expect me to do?' she shouted, throwing her arms up, as if the idea of her paying for a taxi for her own daughter was completely unreasonable.

In the end, our neighbour offered to take us in her car. Mum didn't like that either; I knew she didn't like the street knowing our business. Now the neighbour was in on the whole scandal. When we got out of the car, in the hospital car park, I was expecting Mum to explode on me. Instead, she was unnervingly calm. She opened doors for me, ushered me along, and even carried my hospital bag. And all through the final throes of the labour she was the most supportive and the kindest she had ever been. It was almost as though someone else had stepped into her personality.

'Can I get you anything, love?' she asked. 'A drink? An extra blanket?'

Perhaps it was another false show of unity to impress the midwives. Or maybe she was worried about me breaking down and telling them the truth. But I hoped, and wanted so much to believe, that finally, finally, she wanted to do something good. She had ruined her daughter, completely and irreparably, but perhaps she could redeem herself, in the smallest of ways, with her new grandchild. The pain became unbearable, ripping through my entire body, and I screamed uncontrollably.

'I can't do this!' I wailed. 'I can't!'

A Family Secret

I found myself reaching, instinctively, for Mum's hand. The same hand that had forced its way inside me and left me sobbing in pain and abject humiliation. But now I grabbed onto it like a lifeline. I was given an epidural, but that made the pain stop so suddenly, almost as if it had been switched off at a tap, and it scared me even more.

'Push, push,' urged the midwives.

'Push what?' I asked.

I had no idea what I was supposed to do. I'd had no antenatal classes, no leaflets from the doctor, not even a word of advice from my mother. I had no feeling below my waist. With my legs in stirrups and anaesthetic running through my veins, I felt almost hallucinogenic. There were three midwives around my bed, all giving instructions and platitudes. But again, it was Mum who I turned to. Mum who wiped my forehead. Mum who I trusted. After all she had done, I needed her. I loved and loathed her in equal measure. And I loathed myself, too, for the paradox.

'Listen to the midwife,' Mum said gently. 'You're doing a great job. He's almost here, darling. You're doing a wonderful job.'

It was as though she had transformed into a proper mother, a decent person. I liked this new improved Mum, but she freaked me out, too. She didn't seem real, somehow.

My baby son was born at 5.15 p.m., 6 October 1984, on Jock's nineteenth birthday. He had been due on John

Wood's birthday; he was born instead on Jock's. And in my child's mind, that sealed the paternity issue. He was meant to be here, to save me. And he was meant to be here, today.

Mum sniffed and said, 'Hold him now, you won't see him again.'

He was laid in my arms and just looking at his tiny scrunched-up features made my heart sing with overwhelming joy and love. I drank him in, greedily, every line on his fingernails, every hair on his head, stored carefully in my memory and in my heart.

'You are wanted, you are loved,' I whispered. 'Don't ever believe anything else.'

I felt his tiny hand curl around my finger and marvelled that something so pure, so divine, could come from such evil. Mum nodded to the midwife and she leaned over the bed and held out her arms for me to hand over my son. I couldn't stretch out my arms. I could not be a part of this. But she took him regardless, and in that crushing moment I realised that I was powerless to stop her. It was as if giving birth had aged me ten years and I saw the world through the eyes of a grown-up, through the eyes of a mother. And only now I could see how ridiculous my plans had been. I couldn't run away with my baby. I couldn't bring him up without a home, on my own. I'd had romantic dreams of running away to London and living on nothing but love and fresh air. I had no baby clothes, no pram, nothing.

For his sake, I had to put my own needs aside and I

had to put his first. That was what being a mummy was all about. Even at fourteen I had grasped that and accepted it. But as the midwife took him from me, she might as well have taken a cleaver to my soul. I felt wretched. Mum went home and I was taken to the ward, my son was taken to the nursery, and we were separated. I lay in bed, unable to move because of the epidural, with arms so empty they hurt. I longed to see him, to hold him, to smell him again. The loss was greater than I could ever have imagined – greater than I could cope with. I had produced the most beautiful baby but he was being snatched away and rejected by the very people who ought to have been welcoming him into our family. My story was ending before the ink was even dry on the first page.

I don't think I slept at all that night. Every few minutes I would call a nurse over and ask how my baby was.

'Is he feeding OK?' I asked anxiously. 'I could take him, if you like, settle him for you.'

The nurses were kind but reluctant to give me too many details; worried no doubt about building me up to smash me down all over again.

'He's doing well,' was all they said. 'Don't fret.'

All night I hoped and prayed that Mum would relent. That a guardian angel might step in. That someone, somewhere, would see my plight and let me keep my son.

'I will give anything to be with my angel,' I whispered fervently, through the dim yellow haze of the hospital night lights.

The next morning, Mum and John Wood visited with my younger siblings. They were sent off to the nursery.

'Go and see the new baby,' Mum told them, obviously keen to get them out of the way.

'My new baby,' I thought angrily. 'My baby. They're allowed to see him, but I'm not.'

But I said nothing. I knew better.

Mum looked hard at me and said: 'We had a long talk last night and we've come to a decision. You can keep this baby as long as we raise him as our own.'

I stared at her as the words sank in:

'As our own.'

That was a stab at my heart. They wanted to take him from me. Claim him as their own. But this was a lifeline. Better than I could ever have hoped for. I knew the answer was yes. Yes, yes, yes! But I said nothing. Motherhood had made me brave and astute. I had my baby to think of now. I didn't want them bullying him the way they bullied me.

'Why?' I asked. 'Why do you want to bring him up?'

Mum sighed.

'We can't have children, because of your dad's vasectomy,' she said. 'And we think a new baby might save our marriage. We need this. We need a baby of our own.'

I had no way of knowing whether this was true, or what her real motives were. But I was trapped. It was a cruel compromise. I wanted him to be my son. I wanted the world to know. But like most mothers (except my

84

own), I would lay down my life for my child. I knew this was the best offer I was going to get.

'Yes,' I whispered. 'I'll do it.'

'Well, the final decision has to be yours, apparently,' Mum said, through gritted teeth. 'You have to tell the nurses yourself that we're taking him home and you're happy with it.'

There was a desperation in her eyes, and I saw in that moment how much she wanted the baby. My baby. For the first time, I had power over her. I was in control. Well, I would use it wisely. I waited until my family had left, then the minute the ward doors swung shut I shouted for the nurses: 'Bring my baby! Let me see him! I am taking him home!'

Giddy with excitement, awash with gratitude, I held him in my arms and beamed.

'I'm your mummy,' I said to him quietly. 'I always will be. And I'll never let them hurt you.'

Mum and John Wood visited again that night.

'What about a name?' she asked. 'We thought John would be nice.'

Her voice sliced through me. What kind of sick mind would ask a child to call her baby after her rapist? That was rich, even for her. Jock's real name was John too. For me, the name conjured up suffering, pain and despair.

'No way,' I replied. 'He's not being called John.'

I saw a nurse hovering close by, and I knew again I had the power. I could make decisions. I could voice opinions. While I was in hospital I held the baby and I held all the cards.

Wiser, sharper than I had ever been, I knew I had to make the most of it.

'I will choose the name,' I said boldly.

I could hardly believe the words were coming out of my mouth. And I could see that Mum was ready to erupt, like a pressure cooker. But there was nothing she could do.

'Very well,' she said, each word clipped. 'You do as you wish.'

She snatched up her bag and left. That afternoon I ran through a list of names in my head. I wouldn't even consider John, not for a moment. My plan was to stay at home whilst I was too young to live alone. But the moment I was old enough, the second I had enough money, I would leave and get my own place, just me and my baby. There was no way John Wood, or my mother, or Jock, would ever get their hands on my son. I wanted no reminders and no connections. Especially not in his name. But I was struggling to find a name I liked, so I started saying them out loud, slowly, to my baby as he slept in my arms.

'James, Luke, Oliver, Michael, Daniel …'

But he slept on and on. But when I eventually got to 'Christopher' he opened an eye and looked straight at me. That was all the confirmation I needed.

'There, it's Christopher,' I smiled. 'You chose your own name. And you suit it too.'

A Family Secret

I knew, from RE at school, that St Christopher was the patron saint of travellers, and to me that seemed quite apt.

'You and me are going on a journey through life together,' I smiled. 'I will be with you, every step of the way.'

All thoughts of Jock and his St Christopher medal were far from my mind. Nothing could intrude on the happiness and the unspoilt beauty and innocence of those first few days. We came home from hospital ten days later, on my fourteenth birthday. After that first day of separation, I'd had nine days of pure bliss on the ward with him. And now I was bursting with pride as I carried him through the front door and into the living room of my home. My siblings crowded round, fussing over him and admiring him. For once, I wasn't in trouble. I wasn't shunned or abused. It was the best birthday of my life. In fact, it was the best day of my life so far. I was running out of superlatives in my head. I was literally overflowing with joy. Mum had got me a second-hand Moses basket and a pram. There was a pile of baby clothes, nothing new, mostly donated. I didn't choose a thing. But that didn't matter at all.

'You look so beautiful in everything you wear,' I told Christopher, gently touching the tip of his nose.

And to my surprise, Mum nodded and smiled.

'He does, you're right,' she agreed. 'He is gorgeous.'

I loved the pram, an old-fashioned, bottle-green Silver Cross model, which squeaked as I pushed it along.

I even liked the squeak; it felt as though the pram was proudly announcing Christopher's presence and heralding his arrival: 'Here I come, here I am, with my beautiful new baby.'

Upstairs Christopher slept in his basket, downstairs he was in the pram. But he was so rarely in either; there was always someone holding him or playing with him. I was moved into the box bedroom, which had once been Jock's, and Christopher slept in there with me. Despite Mum's initial vow to steal him away, I did everything for him. He was my baby. I made up the bottles, changed the nappies, washed the bibs and gave him all the love. I cuddled him every spare moment of the day. For the first time ever, my books lay unopened, stacked under my bed.

I no longer needed an escape, a way out. All I needed was right here, in the Moses basket. During the night, long after his bottle was finished, I would sit and look at Christopher and wonder at how lucky I was. Silently and solemnly, I thanked whoever it was who had picked me out for such happiness. And it seemed to spread through the entire family, too.

Christopher had brought the first taste of joy to our house that I could remember. He was a shaft of bright light, a small bundle of joy and of hope. The tension was gone. The arguments stopped. The abuse almost felt like another lifetime. I buried it away as I concentrated on my little boy. Christopher was the focal point of all our lives, but for me he represented life itself. Everything I had, everything I did, every time I breathed, it was all for him. I didn't think too far ahead into the future. I had a day-by-day approach, like most fourteen-year-olds.

To say I was happy just didn't come close. I was in paradise. I had cried myself to sleep for as long as I remembered, but now I lay awake in bed, watching Christopher in the basket at my side, marvelling at the perfection. He was a noisy sleeper and made adorable twittery sounds, like a baby bird. Listening to those funny little snuffles, watching his eyelids flutter as he dreamed, I felt awash with contentment and satisfaction. It didn't matter where he had come from or what had gone before. All that mattered now was the promise and possibility of what lay ahead. It almost seemed that going through the abuse was a trade-off for having Christopher. I'd suffered appallingly, but now the balance had been redressed. I didn't dwell on the evil of his conception. I concentrated only on the miracle of his birth. And one thing was certain: this baby was not Jock's or John Wood's or my mother's. He was mine.

Soon after we came home from hospital, Jock came to visit, bringing with him a belated fourteenth birthday card for me. By now he was living with his new girlfriend and her family, and she came along with him. When I heard his voice in the hallway, my stomach flipped unpleasantly. I had not been looking forward to this meeting, yet I knew it had to happen. Everyone, as usual, was fussing over Christopher, so it was only natural for Jock to peer into the pram and marvel at him too.

'Can I pick him up and hold him?' Jock asked hesitantly.

'Course you can, he's your nephew,' Mum replied, before I even had the chance to open my mouth.

It was like she was waiting, ready, with her answer, as though she sensed I might speak out of turn. I even felt I could hear a slight emphasis on 'nephew', but nobody else seemed to notice it. And anyway, if they had, they would never have dared to say anything. Jock cradled Christopher in his arms and talked softly to him for what felt like a long time. I had never seen him so enraptured, and so gentle and soothing, too. As I watched, split-second flashbacks of the rapes played, like grainy films, across the back of my brain. The brute force of the attacks jarred starkly with the tenderness he showed Christopher. His son. I knew then, beyond all doubt, that he was the father. Christopher looked just like Jock. But Jock looked very much like me, too, so the resemblance was possibly familial, rather than paternal. But when he held him, I could sense it. It almost prickled across the room like electricity. It was almost like a tell-tale whisper, in the air.

'Jock is the father, Jock is the father …'

I could not tell whether he felt it, whether he knew too. It was such a powerful surge and I wondered whether anyone else had noticed – did Mum and John

Wood know? I still wasn't sure they even knew Jock had continued raping me.

Jock eventually handed Christopher back to me and, as our arms touched briefly, I felt dizzy with confusion. We were brother and sister, father and mother, abuser and abused. It was so, so wrong. And yet, as I cradled Christopher, nothing had ever felt more right. I thought that perhaps I was too young to make sense of it and that as I grew older it would become clearer. Little did I know that there was no explanation, no rationalisation, for what had happened to me, and as the years went on it would only get worse.

'I'll be off now,' Jock said awkwardly, his eyes downcast.

I opened my mouth to say goodbye but no words came. And after that moment, in the living room, there was never anything more from him emotionally towards Christopher. I began to doubt the connection I had seen, the bond so strong I could almost have plucked it out of the air and held it.

'You don't need a daddy, you've got me,' I told Christopher. 'I love you enough for both.'

Jock called round on occasion but he never stayed for long and didn't pay Christopher much attention. Mum and John Wood always made it clear that he was not welcome. There had never been any love lost between John Wood and Jock and there was less so now. Mum was infuriated by his rebelliousness, too; she had never been able to control him and squash his spirit, the way she did with me. Jock and I both looked so much like our biological father and I wondered sometimes whether that was why they hated us so much. On those brief visits, Jock showed no special interest in Christopher and we certainly never spoke about him, or about what had gone before. Yet that never bothered me in the slightest. Without the rapes by Jock, I would never have had Christopher. Something so good had come from something so bad.

'I would not change you for the world,' I told Christopher.

And I meant every word of it. My day-to-day routine was so enjoyable, so filled with love, that I no longer needed to cling to the past and pine after what might and what should have been. I slipped into motherhood like it was made for me. My childhood had gone at the age of nine, so I didn't miss it now. For a long time I'd felt out of sync and had no patience with kids my own age. They got on my nerves, in truth. Having Christopher seemed to lend weight and validity to those feelings; I was allowed to feel this way; I was a mother now.

Even though I was made to continue my studies at home, they were now like an afterthought, an inconvenience. My schoolwork had once been the focus of my entire life – now it just got in the way. I would rush through my lessons so that I could take Christopher out in his pram before tea. And whenever I could, I would side-step my schoolwork completely.

'Christopher was up a lot during the night, I need to concentrate on him,' I said. 'I'll keep an eye on him, just for today. My maths can wait.'

Truth was, I was finished with studying. That life was behind me now and I did not miss it at all. At weekends we'd go on long walks. I jumped at the opportunity to show him off. Our neighbours were forever stopping me to look in the pram and admire him.

'Well, hasn't he grown,' they'd smile.

'Isn't he bonny …'

'Ooh, such a happy little thing.'

It made my heart swell with pride. People were very sympathetic and kind – to my face, at least. Everyone knew full well he was mine. Mum's idea to pass him off as her own had been hopeless. The bond between Christopher and me was so strong, it was undeniable. She could never have claimed him as her son. Perhaps people were fascinated because I was such a young mother, and they wanted to have a nosey at the teenager with the baby, wanted to check how I was coping and pick up any snippets of gossip. Or maybe they felt genuine sympathy for me, having sensed or suspected something of our family situation and my ordeal. I was learning, slowly, that not everyone was as wicked and as cynical as my own parents. Either way, I lapped up the attention, and so did Christopher. I loved discussing his sleeping schedule or his upset tummies or his night-time bottles with other mummies. When he smiled for the first time, I announced it to everyone. I was spilling over with excitement.

'It's probably just wind, he's too young to smile,' Mum said, but she had an indulgence about her that I'd never seen before.

I didn't mind whether it was wind or not. Nothing could dent my happiness.

One day, when Christopher was about three weeks old, I went out on some errands, but my pram was too big to fit inside the shop door. I couldn't leave him outside, not even for a minute, so I scooped him up and we went into the shop together.

'I've been waiting for you,' smiled the lady behind the counter. 'I've been looking forward to meeting your lovely boy.'

She handed me a bag with a knitted cardigan and bootees inside. I was so touched that my eyes welled with the ready emotion of a new mum. She hardly knew me, we had never spoken before today, but she had clearly heard about Christopher and wanted to show me some kindness. It was just a small gesture, but I knew I would never forget it.

'Thank you,' I beamed. 'I really appreciate it, we both do.'

From being someone who did not matter a jot, I had been fast-tracked to a position of meaning and substance, where people went out of their way to show they cared. It was more than just a fresh start or a new chapter. It actually felt like a whole new me. The joys of becoming a mother were somehow helping to wash away the stains of evil in my childhood, and I felt cleansed and new.

'You started all of this,' I told Christopher as we walked back home, with the pram squeaking proudly. 'You've made all of this happen for me.'

If it was warm enough I would sit outside, in our small front garden, either with Christopher on my knee or wrapped cosily in the pram. I was so proud of him, and I wanted to share him with the world. Our lollipop lady lived opposite, and she had always been so lovely towards me, right through my childhood. She had twin daughters the same age as me, and privately she was probably devastated at the thought of a child like me having a baby. But she never judged or criticised. She would always pop her head into the pram and comment on Christopher's beautiful outfits or his soft blankets.

'You're doing a fantastic job, Maureen,' she smiled. 'You should be proud of yourself.'

Incredibly, Mum showed Christopher what seemed like genuine affection. Though it amazed me, I welcomed her change of heart. I wanted a calm and loving environment for my baby. And I was grateful that she was so accepting of him. Often when I went out she would come with me. Perhaps she was keeping me in check, in case I said something I shouldn't, but she seemed to really care. She adored Christopher in a way that she had never loved any of her own children. I had never thought she had it in her.

Even John Wood seemed to like having him around. He would happily take his turn with a cuddle. I could not fathom it, but I took it for what I hoped it was. It occurred to me that perhaps John Wood thought the baby was his. Or maybe he was trying to win me over, through Christopher, to make sure I didn't spill my secrets. But my explanation was that Christopher had brought magic into our home. He had brought with him purity, innocence, happiness and love. His birth was like fairy dust sprinkled on each of us.

Chapter 7

It was 2 November, and Christopher was three weeks and six days old.

'You'll be four weeks old tomorrow,' I told him with a smile. 'A whole month!'

The time had flown by, and yet, in many ways, I could not remember what life was like before his arrival. The day was uneventful; I did some washing and pegged his tiny bibs and babygros across a makeshift washing line in the kitchen. We had a walk outside, though it was grey and chilly, and so Christopher was well wrapped up. Early in the evening we found ourselves alone in the house, and I fed and winded him, and changed his nappy, before laying him down in his pram in the living room for a sleep.

'Mummy's going for a bath,' I told him with a smile. 'I won't be long, my beautiful angel.'

Christopher gurgled contentedly. He settled well, as he always did. I'd already run a bath whilst he was feeding so I wasn't long upstairs at all; twenty minutes at the most. As I made my way back downstairs to check on him, I was already looking forward to seeing his sleeping face and his tiny, curled-up fists. But as I reached the bottom of the stairs I was struck by the deathly silence. There were none of the baby bird sounds Christopher always made as he slept. No grunts. No soft murmurings. And I knew there was something dreadfully wrong.

My throat tightened. A feeling of icy dread, starting at the base of my spine, crept up the back of my pyjamas. Standing in the doorway of the living room, I froze for a moment. My hand gripped the door handle. The silence was so powerful, it was almost like a wall, pushing me back. I was too scared to move. And too scared to stand still. But in the next minute I was running over to his pram, saying his name, over and over.

'Christopher, Christopher,' I pleaded. 'Wake up, angel, wake up.'

Desperately, I tapped his foot and touched his face. I leaned over him, pleading with him, begging him to stay with me. But his lips had a bluish tinge and the warmth was already draining from his skin. And I knew that I had lost him. I knew that my own heart, like his, was lost. In terror, I ran screaming from the house, across the road, to hammer on doors. No answer, no answer, it felt like a lifetime, it was taking me hours to find help … But at the next one, the door opened.

'Christopher isn't breathing!' I gasped. 'Help me!'

A Family Secret

I was hysterical. Betty, our neighbour, called an ambulance and ran into our house to begin CPR. I didn't want to look, didn't want to be there, didn't want the stomach-turning confirmation of what I already knew was true. I was aware of flashing blue lights in the street, of my family arriving home, of people crying and shouting and screaming.

'It can't be true! He can't be dead! Not Christopher!'

Even John Wood sat at the dining table, with his head in his hands, and wept. It was the only show of emotion I had ever seen from him and this was confirmation, not that any was needed, of the cataclysmic impact of Christopher's passing.

'So sorry, so sorry,' everyone said.

But nothing could ease my pain. The hours passed in a blur. I felt as though I had been torn in two. As though my heart itself was sobbing. Christopher's tiny body was taken away but I wasn't allowed to go in the ambulance.

'Let me go with him,' I pleaded. 'He's my boy.'

I felt as though my own internal organs were being wrenched from me. I couldn't bear to see him go, all on his own. A doctor was called and I was sedated, and I slept fitfully, in tortured fragments, for the next few days. Each time I awoke, with a start, I would stare at the empty Moses basket beside me and the full horror would come flooding back.

The hospital said they would need to do a post-mortem, and I couldn't bear to consider that someone – a stranger – was cutting into my perfect little boy. It didn't seem dignified or respectful. Yet I also desperately wanted to know how he had died.

'It was cot death *apparently*,' Mum said, in a voice laden with doubt and accusation.

I didn't know what she meant at all. I didn't know what a cot death was either. He had seemed so perfectly well and healthy just minutes before his death. It was completely senseless. Later that week she insisted that we go to the Chapel of Rest to see him, even though I begged not to. I couldn't face it. I needed to remember my boy as he was before.

'You're coming and that's that,' Mum said. 'You're the one who insisted on being a mother. You can take the flack now.'

When we went inside, my baby boy was lying in a tiny coffin, alabaster pale and still. So still. He was dressed in a white outfit, which I hadn't chosen and didn't even recognise.

'Hello, angel,' I whispered softly.

Around his neck he wore a necklace that I recognised as belonging to Jock; one side was a medal of St Christopher, the other a picture of Mary with the baby Jesus. Again, that must have been Mum's decision. It certainly hadn't been mine. In that moment I had a violent flashback to the medal dangling over my face, glinting in the sunlight above the tall ferns, as Jock grunted and thrusted above me. And now the same medal was around my baby son's neck. Our baby son's neck. It was madness. Madness in its purest form. Yet what was pure about it? I leaned forward, with my hand outstretched, and in a split-second of insanity I was almost persuaded that if I could touch Christopher I might be able wake him.

'You can't go near him,' Mum barked.

I froze and then watched, numb, as one of my sisters leaned forward to stroke his face. I didn't understand why she was allowed to touch him, and not me. Why did I have no say in what he wore? And why on earth was he wearing a necklace belonging to the man who had raped me?

The power had shifted back to them now. I had no voice, no opinion. Without Christopher I didn't matter any more. Not one bit. My sister moved his hat a little and it revealed a fresh scar on his head, from the post-mortem. It broke my heart to think of anyone hurting him, and especially on his poor little head.

'My angel,' I whispered.

On one of our happy outings (and how long ago they seemed now), I had saved up and bought Christopher a baby rattle – one big round ball with three or four balls spinning around it, all of different colours. It was the only thing I had ever bought for him myself, and as we were leaving the Chapel of Rest I slipped it discreetly into the coffin, with him. It was the only thing he would have from me. My only contribution to his entire funeral. Saying goodbye was like handing over my own heart. I felt as though I would never feel whole again. Outside, I broke down, and I wept all the way home.

'I don't know why you're crying,' Mum spat. 'We all know you did it. He was fine when we went out, and dead when we got home. Doesn't take a brain box to work out what happened.'

I was reeling. There was no sense at all to her accusations. The post-mortem had clearly shown there was no foul play, no evidence I had harmed him. I could never have hurt Christopher. I adored him. She had simply reverted back to her usual vicious, twisted self. Back at home, she continued to spout bile about me, and the rest of the family followed her lead, as always.

'You're a horrible bitch,' they said. 'You smell. Get a bath.'

I could not leave my bedroom without someone making a jibe or throwing in a nasty remark. Mum's allegations hung over me, circling my head like black crows, waiting to swoop down and pluck out my eyes. But their cruelty did not hurt as much as it might have. I was so locked in grief, so overpowered by my loss, that I hardly heard their words. It was as though everyone around me was talking under water; little made much sense. And they had never supported me anyway. So why start now?

I was totally cut out of the funeral plans. Mum went to see the priest on her own. The Catholic priest refused to bury Christopher because he was born out of wedlock and had not been baptised. I had wanted to have him christened, but he had passed away before it could be arranged. Mum came home and downloaded all her anger onto me, as though it was my fault I hadn't been married when I was raped.

'See the mess you've caused, you filthy little cow,' she hissed.

The next day she went to see the Methodist minister instead, and he proved to be more obliging. Mum was not a churchgoer, and now, I think, the funeral was more about her saving face than following any religious beliefs she had. She wanted to be seen to be doing the right thing. And that was as far as it went.

There were added complications with the burial, too, because there was a gravediggers' strike on at that time, so members of the army were drafted in to help out digging graves. But again, that was none of my business, according to Mum.

'You keep your nose out,' she said.

She chose his flowers: a blue and white wreath with a picture of St Christopher in the centre. I could not even choose the flowers for my own son. My boy's funeral was planned as though I didn't exist. I comforted myself that he had his rattle, but that was the only decision I had made, and even that was in secret. The little rattle, hidden under his blanket, was the only reminder that he was mine. On the morning of the funeral, Jock arrived at the house and announced with his usual arrogance:

'I would like to carry the coffin.'

'I don't think so, lad,' replied John Wood.

They began arguing and I walked into the next room and stared desolately out of the window. But in the background I could hear them shouting and swearing. It didn't seem right, on the day Christopher was being laid to rest. Where was the respect for his short life? As usual with them both, it was about one-upmanship. It was all about being top dog.

'I'm the man of this house,' Jock yelled. 'I should carry it.'

'I'm the head of the family,' John Wood shouted. 'You don't even live here.'

It grew nasty and I could tell they were shoving each other about. By now, Jock was taller than John Wood and much stronger. I knew a fight would end badly for John Wood. I wondered whether the real trigger for their clash was the issue of Christopher's paternity. And if Jock was so insistent on carrying the coffin, surely he had realised, as I had, that he was Christopher's father? Yet, as usual, I simply listened and kept my mouth shut. But then my mother came downstairs and silenced them both.

'Keep your mouths shut,' she told them. 'People will talk. You're not carrying the bloody coffin, Jock, don't be ridiculous.'

In the end, the undertakers carried the coffin, a tiny little wooden box with a simple cross on it. The church was unfamiliar to me; usually I associated these places with calm and healing, but today I had to force myself down the aisle, with leaden feet. There was one hymn, but no readings. There was nothing to mark how special Christopher had been, and how monumental his death would always be for me. I felt as though he had been cheated, let down.

Outside, at the grave, it poured down. I had read about pathetic fallacy in my novels, where the weather follows the mood of the characters, and today it felt as though the angels themselves were weeping.

I was soaked to the skin, I had a thin, useless coat on, but I hardly noticed. My teeth were chattering already from the shock, and the cold simply could not touch me. People lined the path, all the way from the church to the grave. He had been loved by so many, but that was a tiny comfort. For as his coffin was lifted into the ground I wanted to throw myself in too.

Mum had invited mourners back to the house afterwards, and I hung around in the kitchen, staring at my shoes, feeling like a spare part. My whole family seemed to have forgotten that I was Christopher's mother. Or perhaps that was just what they wanted me to think. Some people were kind and did their best to comfort me.

'He was a lovely boy,' said Betty, our neighbour. 'I am so sorry, my love.'

Others looked uncomfortable and didn't know what to say. And one man said to me: 'You are only young. At least this means you can get on with your life, without this shame.'

I gulped. It was as though he thought Christopher's death was a welcome event, a convenient get-out clause for me. I couldn't believe he could be so crass. Horrified, I ran to my room and wept into my pillow.

I heard Mum's footsteps thundering along the landing after me, and as she burst into my bedroom she began hitting me, over and over. Cowering on the bed, I didn't even try to defend myself. I didn't ask her to stop. I no longer cared. A world without Christopher was not a world I wanted to be in.

'Look at me!' Mum ordered in a voice that was no more than a low hiss. 'I want the truth. Who is the father? Which one?'

In that earth-shattering moment I had confirmation that she knew. She knew all about the abuse from Jock. Had she been in on it all from the start? It felt like yet another twist of the knife in my wounded soul.

'Well?' she demanded, her voice quiet and controlled. 'Who is it?'

'I don't know,' I mumbled.

She sat on me and hit me again and again, pinning my arms down with her knees. And then, from the corner of my eye, I saw my bedroom door open and close again quickly. It happened so fast, I had no idea who was on the other side, but it was enough to stop the punches. Mum gave me one last look of sheer disgust and left the room. People use the term 'hell on earth' flippantly, but for me it was right there, in that house.

That night, I talked to Christopher through the lonely hours until dawn.

'Mummy will be with you again soon, my angel,' I

promised. 'I'm still thinking of you, every second of every day.'

And in the days that followed I visited his grave every day. I would sit there for hours on end, staring at the huge mound of earth that covered my baby son. I talked constantly to him, hoping against hope that he might talk back. Each night, when it grew dark, someone would come from home to take me back. I went compliantly, like a zombie, yet knowing I would escape again the minute I got the chance.

I hated being in the house, more than ever. I could see Christopher's pram, trundling and squeaking along the street. I could hear the sweet, snuffly little noises he made as he slept. And I could smell his fresh baby skin close to mine. In every room in the house there were small reminders. And they choked me and comforted me, all at once. I longed to see him. I was desperate to feel him. Yet I was haunted by his ghost, too. I would dream that he was crying, and that I was searching the house for him over and over, trying to find the source of the noise.

'I'm coming, Christopher, I'm coming,' I called.

But the crying grew louder and more insistent and I worried that he was in pain, that he needed me urgently. And then I would wake with a jolt in my empty, lonely bedroom, and realise with cruel and ruthless repetition that he was gone. I was grieving for him, over and over again, and it exhausted me, physically and mentally.

Desperate for peace, I stayed out of the house for

longer and longer periods. Once, I ran away and walked round and round the graveyard until the early hours of the morning. I had no intention of going back home, but then I missed Christopher, and the smell of him, and the small indentation his tiny head had made on the mattress in his Moses basket. I longed to be close to where he had once been. When I finally made my way back home, and silently let myself in through the back door, nobody had even missed me. There didn't seem to be anyone who had noticed how destitute and hopeless I felt. Without Christopher, it was as if nothing I had seemed to matter. It was as though a part of me had physically died with him and I was now existing, in a half-life, hovering behind death's curtain, waiting to pass to the other side.

Chapter 8

I thought the abuse was over. There had been nothing following the confirmation of my pregnancy, over six months earlier. It was the one small chink of light in a dark world, although it did little to lift my spirits. But just a few weeks after Christopher's funeral I found myself alone in the house with John Wood.

I was in my bedroom talking silently to Christopher, with my eyes shut tight and my cheeks wet with tears. When the door opened and John Wood stood towering in the frame, I felt no immediate sense of foreboding. After all this time, I was not expecting anything bad. But in the next second he lunged at me, his eyes blazing, as he shoved me, hard, against the headboard. There was no build-up. No warning. He raped me there and then, more violently and more forcefully than I could ever remember before.

There was spit flying from his lips, sticking in my hair, and his breath, sour and angry, made me heave. I could feel my arms bruising under his grip. It was as though he was trying to cause me as much pain and fear as he could. I felt like I had been brutally attacked by a complete stranger. This rape, somehow, was different. It was over quickly, but I knew the scars would last a lifetime. He slammed out of the room, wiping his mouth with the back of his hand and smoothing down his pointy little beard. He didn't say a single word. He didn't even bother threatening me to keep quiet. He probably knew by now that there was no need. I was petrified – literally. It was as though I had been turned to stone and I could not move for the rest of the day. I could not even cry. And it came to me, in the hours afterwards, that this rape had been a punishment. This was his form of retribution. He hated me because Christopher was dead. Like my mother, he blamed me. It was like I had been steamrollered; I felt flattened and hollow. I was completely finished, not only as a mother, but as a human being also. In the days after the rape I struggled even to speak. And underneath my grief bubbled an intense fury. I kicked back against life and all the shit it had thrown at me. I had always enjoyed going to church, I was a committed Christian, but now I turned vehemently against God and religion.

'What kind of God takes away a baby?' I asked angrily. 'How can it be fair?'

John Wood made his own home brew, which was stored in the outhouse, a little room next to the kitchen. There were bottles and bottles of the stuff, and I knew he and my mother, who both drank heavily, wouldn't miss a few. I began drinking during the night, when the rest of the house was asleep. By the time morning came I was often quite drunk, yet chillingly sober at the same time. I didn't care if I was caught drinking. I didn't care about anything. What on earth could they do to me that was worse than what I had already endured? I wanted so much to be with Christopher, and if dying was what it took, I was prepared for it. I knew my family wouldn't miss me, that was for sure.

Social services came to see me, probably because I was spending so long at the cemetery, and also because I was running away more and more frequently. The social workers had been in and out of our lives since we had come out of care as small children, and now they seemed to take a particular interest in me.

'You're proving quite a handful these days,' said one social worker.

Again, I longed for her to ask me the question. The *right* question. Again, she did not. Instead she decided, after discussion with my parents, that I should be placed in a children's home, for just one week, to be assessed.

'Fine,' I said numbly.

As she drove me to the children's home, she mentioned something about it being good for my parents to have a break too. She was so outrageously far off the mark that I actually laughed. How little she knew.

The children's home was trialling a new technique in behaviour management called 'Pin Down', which involved isolating children and denying them basic privileges. It was like walking into a prison. I wasn't even allowed to leave my room to use the toilet. I had to knock on my door for hours on end to ask permission, and on one occasion the staff left me until I wet myself. It was degrading and humiliating. I couldn't for the life of me see how that was going to help any child to behave well. Years later, the technique was banned and slammed as a controversial experiment. For me, it made little impact, because my thoughts were dominated, constantly, by my grief for my son. And locking me up, or letting me out, made very little difference.

When I returned home, I eventually went back to school full-time, but I no longer had any focus for my studies. The girls in my class would waffle on endlessly about makeup and new clothes and their latest teenage crushes. They were everyday teenage dilemmas.

'Did you get a new dress for Saturday? We're all going out, Maureen, you should come too. Slap a bit of makeup on and enjoy yourself.'

Listlessly, I shook my head. I felt insulted by the trivia. I was angry, deep down, that the world was carrying on as normal. My friends were discussing shades of lipstick whilst I worried about my baby son, decaying under a mound of soil, all alone and crying for his mummy.

And so I became more isolated and alienated than

ever before. Grief stretched out before me and formed a chasm between me and my peers. There was no way back for me as a teenager. No way back for my youth. Instead, I sat on my own, with my sadness. I still worked hard in class and did my best in lessons, especially in English Literature and Home Economics – reading and cooking were often what got me through the day – but my mind was elsewhere so much of the time.

One day another pupil came to me and smirked, 'You're pregnant again, aren't you?'

'No, I am not,' I retorted.

But I heard the rumours again and again.

'They reckon you're having another baby because you're such a slut,' confided one of my friends.

A fury rose within me. I felt that by trashing my character they were also attacking Christopher's memory. I asked around and was dismayed to discover that my closest friend was the source of the lie.

'How could you?' I seethed.

Blinded by rage and convinced somehow that I was defending my son's reputation, I grabbed her hair and threw her to the floor.

'Take it back, you liar!' I yelled.

I knew I was taking my hurt out on her. She didn't deserve quite such a vicious punishment. When I was frogmarched to see the deputy head, I admitted everything. She took me home, and I was suddenly panic-stricken, thinking Mum would explode when she heard, and hit me twice as hard as I'd hit the girl. Instead

Mum stood at the doorway, pursed her lips, and said: 'Well, the girl must have deserved it.'

And that was that. There was no consequence, not even a telling off. School suspended me for a week, and I counted myself lucky. I couldn't fathom Mum's behaviour. She would normally never pass up the opportunity to chastise me. She was consistently inconsistent and unpredictable, which made her all the harder to live with.

Though I no longer had any enthusiasm for school, it was at least a chance to escape the house – and avoid the possibility of finding myself alone with John Wood. Since that brutal attack following Christopher's death, I had tried to make sure we were never in the same room together. I could not bear even to breathe the same air as him. But it was inevitable, with my older siblings leaving home, and Mum working in the evenings, that I would sometimes be in the house on my own with him. I tried to slip out of the house myself, but if I was caught he would always bring me back. And occasionally, I was sure, he would skip work or lie about his shift pattern so that he could take me by surprise and ambush me in my bedroom.

He would walk in, his pale, watery eyes fixed on me through his spectacles, his hand already fiddling with his belt buckle. The anticipation, the dread of what was coming, was chilling. Sometimes my heart would be beating so fast I thought I might drop dead. These days, he didn't speak. He didn't need to. He knew I had no words. On those occasions, when it was just me and him, he never missed a chance to rape me. Sometimes, if he had a week of late shifts, it might happen every day. By the end of that block of shifts I felt as though I had been chewed up and spat out.

I was absolutely powerless, helpless. I couldn't fight back. And I didn't even think about telling anyone. Why would I be believed? Why would anyone, for one moment, take my side? It had never happened before, so it was not going to happen now. Besides, John Wood was an upstanding member of the community, well-respected and well-liked. He had plenty of friends and contacts. I was a wayward, runaway teenager with a pregnancy and a bereavement behind me. And I had no friends, no family, not even a mother who loved me. Nobody cared about me, so why should I care about myself? I had a sense of complete defeat. Losing Christopher had broken me. It was a turning point, and they could no longer reach me or hurt me. I was beyond all that.

The following Mother's Day I awoke with a heavy heart. When I went downstairs into the living room I could immediately sense a charge in the atmosphere. We had always bought gifts for my mother, on John Wood's orders, and this year was no different. I handed Mum the obligatory card and flowers and mumbled: 'Happy Mother's Day.' To my utter confusion, she handed me a card and a small box of chocolates in return. I looked at her, wondering what on earth was going on.

'Open the card,' she goaded. 'Go on, you are a mummy, after all.'

I turned away, my eyes swimming with tears, but she grabbed my arm sharply and said: 'Open it!'

Reading the card, I felt a shiver run through me. She had signed it 'from Christopher'.

'Happy Mother's Day,' Mum cackled, laughing as she watched the tears stream down my face.

I dropped the card like it was a hot coal and ran back to my bedroom. For any parent losing a child is a horrific experience, and the pain does not ease with time. For me, I had lost a child and I had also lost my place as a mother.

After Christopher died, nobody mentioned his name. Nobody ever referred to the fact that I was still a mother, still a parent, albeit a bereaved one. That, too, was snatched away from me. I lost my child, and I lost myself, as a parent. And now the only reference to that time was a sick, sad card from my mother. What sort of deviant witch was she? And what was it about me that made her hate me so much? If I could have sunk any lower, I did so that day.

In 1985, the year after Christopher's death, my family moved house. I kicked against it because I wanted to stay with my memories. I wanted to breathe in the faint reminders of him. But of course, nobody listened to me.

And saying goodbye to the bedroom where he had slept, and the living room where he had died, was agonising.

When everything was packed, I slipped back into the bedroom, empty now and bare, and whispered a final goodbye.

'I'm not going without you,' I promised. 'I won't forget you.'

But my words felt as empty as the room. It seemed as though the world was moving on and leaving him behind. Closing the door, that last time, I felt as though the wounds of my grief were being ripped apart all over again.

The new house served a purpose; there was a bed there to sleep in and of course to be raped in. We might have moved to a new address, but the miasma of evil followed us there. My mother announced my surname would be changed to 'Wood' too. Inwardly, I kicked against it, but in reality there was nothing I could do.

'Maureen Wood,' I repeated dully. 'That's the same name as yours.'

Mum nodded smugly, as though the honour was all mine.

By now, my interest in school had waned completely, and I began missing lessons. I fell in with the other truants and spent most afternoons in the pub, drinking vodka shots and eating crisps. Around that same time, aged fifteen, I met my first boyfriend, Dave, through a school friend. I had absolutely no interest in sex or in boys, but Dave and I got chatting at her house one night, and he was gentle and protective. And at seven years my senior, he made me feel safe. Truth was, I didn't fancy him at all, but I did warm to his personality. He was good to me. And he didn't push me into sex, or any kind of intimacy.

It took six months before our relationship became physical. The first time we had sex we'd been to the pub; both of us probably hoping, for different reasons, that I would have too much to drink. It was no reflection on him that the act itself was, for me, just another tick in a box, and my overwhelming feeling afterwards was of relief. It was consensual, unlike every other encounter I'd ever had. And that probably should have meant more than it did. But by now I was so broken and so damaged that I was beginning to wonder whether I would ever be able to enjoy sex with anyone or whether it was tainted beyond redemption. Poor Dave had no idea about the abuse I'd suffered, so I must have seemed like a puzzle to him. Perhaps he picked up on the weight of unhappiness that hung inside me, permanently, like a stone. For my part, I think I was looking for a way out. A reason to leave home. I saw everyone around me having relationships and settling down, and I decided I should do the same. When Mum finally met him, she curled her lip and said: 'He's far too old for you, Mo-Jo.'

The sickening irony of her statement was possibly lost on her, but not on me. I left school the following summer with just one O Level, in Home Economics. I felt some disappointment, because I had once been one of the brightest students in my class, tipped by my teachers to do well, especially in English. But I had turned my back on the world, just as I felt the world had turned its back on me. Failing my exams felt like a statement, an act of rebellion, which, when the results came through, was something of a damp squib. Still, the O Level in cooking would serve me well. Baking, like reading, was a therapy and a catharsis for me. These were lifelines, and a constancy in my life that real people never were.

I was still only sixteen when Mum went off to Scotland for a fortnight's holiday to visit her relatives, leaving me on my own in the house with John Wood. As the front door slammed shut behind her, he turned to me and said: 'You're my wife this week.'

A chill ran right through my veins. I could almost feel my blood solidifying with the fear. Looking back now, I feel furious at myself that I didn't run away, there and then. But it wasn't that simple. The sixteen-year-old me was frightened of him. Frightened of my mother. I had no idea whether she was in on his little plan; whether indeed her entire holiday had been planned to suit him. And even if I did run away, I knew that I could never truly escape them – they would always catch up with me.

I had very little fight left in me. The only real and lasting escape from the abuse would, I knew, be death. But however much I longed to be with Christopher, I was not prepared to give up on myself or on my life. I didn't think about suicide, I was a survivor, and despite everything I was determined to see it through.

That night, I was on my way up to bed when John Wood grabbed me from behind and threw me roughly against the stairs. He raped me, right there and then, on the staircase. He was so incensed, so savage, that he seemed inhuman. His hands clutched around my throat. His foul beard scratched against my cheeks. I thought, genuinely, that he might kill me. For the first time, I was in fear of my life. When he was done, he stepped over me on the stairs, like I was a piece of rubbish, and went up to the bathroom. I lay there, doubled over, barely able to believe I was still breathing. Stinging with pain, I eventually managed to crawl up to my bedroom, too terrified to stay in the house, and also too terrified to leave it. Never had Christopher and my days as a mummy seemed so far away.

The following morning, at 5 a.m., I had to get up for work. After leaving school, I'd got a job in a factory making electrical components for cars. Like a robot, I brushed my teeth, got dressed, and let myself out of the house as quietly as I could, leaving evil sleeping. After work I came home, cooked an evening meal for John Wood and cleaned the house. I was on auto-pilot, indoctrinated to follow rules. That night, at 10 p.m., he arrived home from work.

'Where's my tea?' he asked.

In his mind he was playing out a sick fantasy of me as his teenage bride, his child wife. And obediently, I complied. After he had eaten, the same, horrific routine began again. He raped me over and over again, the whole night, until it was time for me to go to work the next morning. He didn't sleep, he didn't even seem to get tired. It was as if he was running on a toxic adrenalin; the fix from each rape giving him the energy to launch the next attack.

'Please,' I sobbed. 'I can't take any more.'

But he just grunted and forced my head back. When the dawn came, and I had to go to work, he took himself off to bed. He would not respect my wishes or my body. But he respected my working hours. And oddly, although I could not bring myself to run away during the night, I was able to get myself showered and ready for work, as normal. It was as though my brain had partially shut down, and I could only follow set tasks, without deviation. I was brainwashed, I could no longer think for myself. And John Wood clearly felt so sure of himself, and was so complacent in his domination, that he allowed me to go to work, knowing full well that I would never have the confidence or the impudence to betray his deadly secret.

That morning I was undergoing training, preparing me for clerical work in the office. I had a rotten headache and my mind was elsewhere. I struggled to concentrate properly. Part-way through the session the manager called me into her office. My heart sank. I thought I was in trouble, and I was going to be sacked.

'Maureen, what's wrong with you?' she asked gently.

I stared, uncomprehending. Nobody had ever asked me what was wrong, in my entire life. Nobody had ever directly confronted the problem. And now the moment was here, I was dumbstruck.

'You are covered in bruises and you look pale. In fact, you look terrible,' she said. 'I know there's something wrong and I want to help you. Please tell me.

'Tell me where you got those bruises. Tell me what happened.'

Her kindness overwhelmed me. And, before I could process my thoughts, it all tumbled out. It was as though I had been waiting all these years, since I was a frightened eight-year-old, for someone to ask what was wrong with me.

'My stepfather has been raping me, it's been going on for years,' I told her, each word tripping over the next. 'He rapes me over and over, he's violent and he's angry and I think he's going to kill me one of these days.'

The words gushed out in a torrent. It was like a dam bursting. And as I spoke, and as I sobbed, I felt lighter and lighter. By the end of my unburdening I was almost floating.

'Where's your mum?' she asked, with tears streaming down her cheeks too. 'Where's the rest of your family?'

I clamped shut again. Blocked. The abuse by Mum was unthinkable. Unspeakable. It felt like the last taboo and I couldn't begin to admit it out loud. I didn't even want to admit it to myself.

'She's on holiday,' I mumbled. 'They won't help me.'

'I'm going to call social services,' said the manager eventually. 'We need to get some help for you.'

She rang social services, as I waited in the office, then she drove me to the offices herself that same day. I was filled with gratitude at her kindness, but I found it puzzling too. Why would anyone want to help me? The manager, whoever she was, had changed my life. She had most likely saved my life. And yet I didn't even know her name. When she dropped me off, she put her hand on mine and said:

'Good luck, Maureen. It will get better from here.'

And then, she was gone. Inside, the social worker took me into a small room, opened up a file, and said: 'I believe you have made an accusation of sexual abuse.'

'It is not an accusation,' I replied. 'It is just what happens to me.'

'Would you like to make a report to the police?' she asked.

I shook my head firmly.

'Definitely not,' I replied.

I could not go through that. I couldn't face more examinations, more trauma. I didn't want to bring more trouble into my family. I wanted an escape.

'I just want out,' I said desperately. 'Please get me out of that house.'

The social worker nodded and left the room for a few minutes. When she returned, she said:

'I've found you a place in supported accommodation, but you can't move in immediately. You will have to go to meetings with the other residents to be approved, and you will also have to agree to counselling by the NSPCC.

How does this sound to you? Can you hold on until then?'

I nodded. This was the start. The start of the end of my suffering.

That night I was petrified to go home but I had nowhere else to go. The rapes continued for the rest of the week; sometimes the attacks lasted all night. He seemed to take perverse delight in knowing we had the house to ourselves, and he raped me when and wherever he chose. He even raped me the night before Mum was due home from Scotland. She must have known, when she walked in through the door, that I was traumatised. I was covered in bruises and pinch marks. I was painfully thin, desperately pale, and exhausted to the point of collapse. If a total stranger – my manager – could spot it, then surely my mother would notice?

'Have you behaved yourself?' she asked me, looking instead at her husband for confirmation.

He said nothing, but his smile said it all. I had no idea if she knew. She had never once touched me since I'd fallen pregnant with Christopher, but I couldn't believe that she hadn't worked out what was going on. That week she and John Wood had a terrible row, and I heard her scream:

'Admit it! You prefer fucking her to me! You prefer fucking my daughter!'

For me, it was the confirmation I didn't want. She knew he was still raping me. And now, as if things couldn't get any more absurd, she was jealous of me. I was causing trouble in their marriage. It was so surreal and so sick, it was almost comical.

Secretly, I went to the weekly meetings at the new house and I got on well with the other residents. They were around my age and a little older. Like me, they'd had their problems at home, though I doubted many had come from families quite like mine. During those final few weeks that I lived in the family home, John Wood never touched me once. It was strange and baffling, the way he just stopped abusing me. I can only think that I had a confidence about me, and an indifference to him and to my home life, and he had picked up on that. It was as though I was giving off a strange scent, warning him off. I was no longer a soft target, no longer a willing victim. I was on my way up. I answered back to him and Mum.

'Make us a drink, Mo-Jo,' she would say.

'I'm busy, I'll do it later,' I heard myself reply.

I was amazed by this new me, and I quite liked her too. I slacked on my chores. I stayed out late. My relationship with Dave petered out, but we were on friendly terms. Though not exactly carefree, I was feeling better and brighter than I had for a long time. The house meetings went well too. Whatever the basis, I bonded with the other teenagers there, and when they gave me a set of keys I felt like singing for joy. I skipped home, with keys – my keys – in my pocket. That feeling of independence was priceless. I felt weightless.

'Where the hell have you been?' Mum demanded. 'It's 9 p.m. and you were supposed to cook our tea.'

'I'm moving out,' I announced, unable to keep the smile off my face.

She stared at me, trying to weigh up for a moment whether or not I was lying.

Then she snapped: 'Pack your fucking bags and go now. Get out of my house!'

John Wood stepped in and tried to stop me, to persuade me to change my mind. He was less hot-headed, less impulsive than my mother. But he was also more intelligent. I knew he would be thinking ahead.

'Think about what you're doing, Maureen,' he said, with a warning note in his voice.

He was trying to scare me. But I knew, deep down, it was more likely that he was scared. Scared of losing his sexual punchbag. And more scared that I might open my mouth.

The argument raged until 1 a.m. Eventually I managed to escape to my room and I packed all my stuff, what little I had. It didn't add up to much for sixteen years of life. I had a few tracksuits, jeans and trainers. Books. My wonderful books. My rosary beads. And that was it. I didn't have a single photo of Christopher. Mum had seen to that. After his death she had packed away everything that was associated with him and I was not allowed even to keep one of his tiny little hats or a pair of mittens. It was like a punishment; she confiscated his clothes, his pram and all reminders of him, because she knew that I longed to see them and smell them again. Years later, when I plucked up courage to ask her again for a memento, she snapped: 'I threw the lot away. There's nothing left.'

With all my worldly goods in three carrier bags, I sat on the bed, swinging my legs, and waited until 5 a.m., when I knew the first buses would begin. Then I crept downstairs, as quietly as I could, and let myself out into the crisp morning air. I had walked out. I was never going back. I was free.

Trudging down the main road, dragging my bags along the pavement, I suddenly heard a car slowing down, behind me. For a wild moment I panicked, thinking John Wood and Mum had sent someone to abduct me and take me back. But it was a police car, and an officer wound down the window and said: 'Where are you going on your own at this hour?'

I explained I was leaving home, and they offered me a lift.

'No, thank you,' I said, polite but wary.

I wanted to do this myself. And I was worried, even at this stage, that they might take me home. Instead, they followed me, slowly, down the street, and watched as I climbed onto the bus, before driving off. It was another small slice of kindness that I would remember, always.

I was bursting with anticipation on that bus ride. I gazed out of the grimy windows as we passed shuttered-up shops and houses in darkness; here and there I spotted a light on, curtains open. The world was slowly waking up, and so was I. Sure, I had no idea of what was ahead. But I knew it had to be better than what I had left behind. Little did I know I could not shake off the past like a dirty old coat.

Chapter 9

For the next few months my life was wonderfully normal and predictable. Like most teenagers my age, I had no idea how to budget. I had to learn how to do a weekly shop and how to organise myself. In those early weeks I blew my entire week's money on a night out and had to live on toast for the next six days.

'We all did it, Maureen,' laughed one of my housemates.

But I soon learned how to be sensible. And I loved cooking, which was a bonus, for me and my housemates. I rustled up lots of cheap basic meals, casseroles, pies, cakes and biscuits.

'This is great,' they said. 'You should be a chef.'

It was peculiar to be appreciated and popular, but I was enjoying it. We lived in a large, Victorian, three-storey building in Stoke-on-Trent town centre, where I had my own bedroom, with a shared living room, kitchen and dining room. The place was clean; spotless in fact.

And it was warm too. But more than anything, it was safe. For the first time, I felt truly safe. I could close my bedroom door and know that nobody would walk through it without my permission. For me, that was groundbreaking. I attended group counselling, as part of my agreement with social services. We all sat in a circle and I felt horribly awkward and exposed.

'Could you draw a picture of your feelings?' asked the counsellor.

I looked blankly at her. Where on earth would I start? That would be a hell of a picture. It was no reflection on the counsellor, but really, she had no idea how to help me. I continued with the sessions, just to fulfil my part of the bargain, but I gave nothing away.

Around a month after moving into my new home I bumped into an old school friend in town. I had known she was gay, right through school, so when she asked if she could come back to my flat I had an idea what she was planning. I was sitting on my bed, nervously making small talk, when she kissed me. And in that moment I realised I much preferred kissing girls to boys. I had not even considered it until then. We didn't see each other again after that night. I wasn't ready for any kind of relationship, with anyone, but our time together was a memory I would always treasure; it was a small piece of the jigsaw which, when complete, would be the finished me.

I couldn't face going back to the factory where I had worked. I felt certain that everyone would know about me being taken into the office, and driven away to see social services, and that they would all be whispering behind my back.

'That's her, the one whose stepdad raped her. Did it for years, she reckons …'

I still couldn't shake the conviction that the abuse was my fault, and I was just too ashamed to return to my job. I didn't even go back to thank the manager, which is one of my biggest regrets. I owed her more than she could probably ever imagine. But I was young and troubled, and I hope that she understood.

One of the requirements of living at my new house was that I must be working or studying, and so I enrolled to study hairdressing. I worked in a salon five days a week with one day in college, and I loved it. In the evenings I would go to the pub if I had enough money, otherwise I'd spend my time alone, in my room. And if I was honest, I preferred being on my own. On one night out I bumped into Dave, my first boyfriend. He and I had drifted apart as I coped with the abuse at home, but we settled back into a relationship easily enough. Dave was familiar and he represented safety to me, but again, what I longed for most were the nights on my own. Christopher was always in my thoughts and I liked to be alone with them. I drank heavily to blot out my grief, but alcohol only made it worse. Clouds of depression hung low over me and I knew they always would. I had to learn to live with them, somehow.

During office hours there was a welfare officer based in our house, and she insisted I write to Mum and tell her where I was living. It was, apparently, one of the rules, to keep parents informed. I did as she said, scribbling a simple note with my address, but as I posted it I dreaded the consequences. My only comfort was that my new place was a good half hour's bus journey from my old family home and I didn't think Mum would be bothered to make the effort. Several months on, one autumn day, the welfare officer tapped at my door and said: 'Maureen, you have a visitor. Well, two in fact.'

My blood ran cold. I knew instantly it had to be her. Yet she'd given me no warning at all. I went downstairs, all at once a shivering, frightened shell of myself. I had regressed ten years in a matter of seconds. Just seeing her in the hallway gave me a real fright. I worried, for a moment, that she might force me to go back home. She had brought one of my sisters with her and also my old black-and-white portable TV from home. It was a little old-fashioned set, with a dial to change channels.

'Well, look where you've been hiding,' said my mother, as though she had caught me out, as though she had the upper hand already.

I felt sure now that she was here to drag me home. Instead, it turned out that she wanted me to go for dress fittings with my sister. She was getting married the following spring and I, along with a clutch of other girls, was to be a bridesmaid.

'You need to be at the bridal shop next Saturday,' Mum told me. 'If you're not there I'll be round here and there'll be trouble.

'It's her big day. We don't need you ruining everything.'

She plonked the telly down on my chest of drawers with such force, I thought she might smash the screen. I didn't understand why she had brought it for me. There had to be something in it for her, but I didn't know what.

They didn't stay for long, thankfully, but for ages after they'd left I just couldn't settle. And though I should have been pleased with the telly, as I didn't have one, I hated it. It was black and white, and yet it reminded me, in sharp focus, of the grisly technicolour horrors of home. It almost smelled of home. I couldn't bring myself to even switch it on. But I knew better than to cross my mother, so the following weekend, as instructed, I made my way to the bridal shop. I spotted John Wood from way down the street. He was standing outside, a small, slightly stooped man, his spectacles and his beard and his thin, mean chin, clearly in profile. I hadn't seen him since I'd left home and my stomach did a double turn. Much as I liked to think I was brave and sassy, he still turned my bones to jelly.

'Good morning, Maureen,' he said formally, but I did not reply.

My tongue was stuck to the roof of my mouth. I was so afraid. I walked straight into the shop and he followed. Because he was paying, he kept a close eye on the budget, but apart from that he had little to say. I tried not to make eye contact throughout the whole session. Even though I was out from under his reach, I had the impression he could pluck me out of my new life, if he desired, and take me back. I felt like a second-hand, soiled possession. And in the days afterwards, with his disgruntled face and his watery eyes fresh in my mind, I relived the terror and the revulsion of the rapes. There were times when I felt I had made no progress at all; how could I live without abuse? Truthfully, I hadn't a clue. This was supposed to be a new start but I didn't even know how to start again. I wanted so badly to feel safe but I was scared witless all of the time – scared that the past might catch up with me, scared of what the future might bring, and scared most of all that the present could be taken away from me.

In January 1988, when I was seventeen, I missed a period and, with the familiar feelings of nausea and exhaustion, I realised that I was pregnant. I felt a swirling mix of emotions; panic, sadness, nostalgia and fear. But above it all, shining through, were feelings of happiness and joy.

'I won't forget you, Christopher,' I promised.

I wanted this baby desperately, but I also found it hard not to think about Christopher in the same breath. Dave was thrilled. This was his first child and, though it wasn't planned, he was over the moon.

'Can't wait,' he beamed.

We moved into a flat together and began preparing for our new baby. For me, each milestone was bitter-sweet. The first time I felt our unborn baby stir, I remembered the fluttery sensations in my belly every time Christopher had moved. And as my bump grew, I was cast back to the last time my body had changed like this, to the last time I had been a mummy. Yet I couldn't deny that I was feeling broody and excited and maternal all over again. This, after all, would be Christopher's brother or sister. He would live on through them, just as he did through me. And this time there was no panic over adoption or abortion. There was nobody to glare over my shoulder and tell me what I was going to do. Even so, I was wary of my mother's reaction. I didn't want her involvement, so I didn't even tell her. A couple of months on, I was relieved to find I could still fit into my bridesmaid's dress for my sister's big day.

The night before the wedding I was summoned back home, to be with the rest of the bridesmaids. My family had moved house again, so it was thankfully not my old bedroom, but nonetheless I felt uneasy. And it was disturbing, sleeping under the same roof as my odious parents. The memories of what they had done to me were crawling out of the walls, like an infestation. I hardly closed my eyes at all that night; it was as if being at home gave me an instant case of insomnia. The following morning, as we did our makeup and curled our hair, I found myself sitting next to Mum. I took a deep breath; she would have to know some time, after all.

'I'm pregnant,' I said quietly.

'What – again?' she said.

I looked her in the eye, telling myself I was not scared, and replied: 'Yes? What's your problem?'

Unusually for her, she had little to say in return, but she shot me a look that said she expected nothing better from me. The day went without any flashpoints, but as soon as I could escape the wedding, I did. I had no plans to see any of my family again.

The pregnancy went well, though I was always on edge, worried something might happen to my baby. Sadly, my relationship with Dave didn't go as smoothly, and towards my final trimester I found myself on my own.

'Give our relationship another chance, Maureen, for the baby,' he pleaded.

At first, I stood firm. But when I went into labour we patched up our differences. I was as anxious as he was to give things another go. We both wanted a proper family, but I knew even then that we were clinging on to something that was already in pieces. Our son, Ben, was born in September 1988, weighing 5lb 11oz. He was long and skinny and looked just like his father. He was not at all like Christopher or me. But even so, Ben's birth brought back all the memories in sharp detail, and at times I saw flashes of Christopher sleeping in my arms, Christopher murmuring in his Moses basket, Christopher silent and pale in his pram, Christopher ghostly in his coffin. For Ben's sake, and for mine, I tried hard to push the comparisons away. I was determined to be a good mother and knew that I had to focus on what I had, not what I had lost. I was filled with hope for the future, but there was anxiety and trepidation too.

A Family Secret

The days passed and, though I didn't want to admit it, I struggled to bond with Ben, because deep down I was expecting to lose him. Deep down, I thought he was on loan, as Christopher had been, and I could not go through that pain again. I couldn't let myself go completely and entirely. I couldn't give everything. And so I held back.

'Mummy loves you,' I told him. 'I'm doing my best.'

But for me, and for him, that wasn't good enough. And I knew that. I was kidding nobody, certainly not myself. When Ben was six weeks old I took him to Scotland to show him off to my relatives. We had a good week, and they made such a fuss of him, but when I got back to Stoke I discovered I had lost my flat and it had been reallocated. I had a new baby and I had nowhere to go. Much as it stuck in my throat, I found myself on my mother's doorstep, pleading for a bed for the night. There was nowhere else I could go at such short notice and I could not risk being homeless with a tiny baby. I was back in the bosom of evil. Back with my maker, and my destroyer.

Looking back, I can see how hard it might be to understand my decision. I can't understand it myself. But that was all I knew. I was still a teenager, with one baby in heaven and one in my arms. I was short on confidence and even shorter on love. I went back to the only family I had ever known.

It was still rocky between Dave and me, but he came to stay with us, temporarily, to help with Ben. Mum loved having a baby in the house again; she transformed once more into a doting grandmother, clucking over the pram, giving cuddles and paying compliments. Sometimes it almost felt like I had gone back in time and Christopher was still alive.

'He's a beautiful boy, Mo-Jo,' she said with a smile. 'Well done.'

And though I hated to admit it, I craved that approval and affection. I wanted a mother. Yes, I loathed her for what she was and what she had done, but I could not escape the fact that she was all I had. At first, I was confused and bewildered by her warmth. She chucked in little snippets of normality, almost as though she was trying to throw me. Or I wondered if perhaps she was trying to impress Dave. It had always been her way, after all, to present a cosmetic front to the world. But then, dangerously, I settled into enjoying and expecting her good will. I let myself believe that this was the real her. She even offered to babysit one night.

'You should go out, let your hair down,' she told us.

That left me speechless. Dave couldn't see what all the fuss was about; he had no idea of the reptile that lurked beneath her outer layer. True to form, a couple of months on, Mum announced that they were moving house, yet again, to a smaller place.

'No room for you,' she said sharply.

And just like that, she was back to her old self. We had outstayed our welcome and it was time to leave. Foolishly, I had become reliant on her and had done

nothing about finding a new flat, and so I found myself
on my own with Ben in a hostel, until I could find something more permanent.

The relationship between me and Dave deteriorated
yet further and we were barely on speaking terms. We
both knew it was time to go our separate ways. Stuck in
one room at the hostel, with a baby to look after, and
with no support and no money, I began to struggle. I was
constantly terrified that Ben was going to die. I would
spend hours trying to settle him, but as soon as he was
asleep I would wake him again to make sure he was OK.
And I dreaded sleeping myself, in case I woke to find him
dead. Images of him white and cold in his cot burned
across my eyes. There was, after all, no explanation for
Christopher's death, so what if it happened to Ben, too?
I convinced myself there could be a genetic fault, and
that Ben, like Christopher, might be cursed. Ben was so
precious to me, I loved him so much, that I could not
allow myself to get too close to him. I knew I would not
cope with losing him, so I had to protect myself.

'He's only on loan,' I reminded myself.

And part of me wondered whether I could or should
open my heart to love another child the way I had loved
Christopher, because he had been everything to me. Was
it a betrayal for me to love another child the same? Was
it tempting fate to give myself completely to this baby,
as I had before? The questions and dilemmas swam
around my head but there were no answers and there
was no solace. I was tormented by my worries; worries

about Ben and worries about my own failings as a mother. I was on edge, all the time. When Ben was around ten months old he went through a severe teething episode, where he screamed relentlessly. Nothing I did seemed to soothe him, and again I blamed my own inadequacies as a mother.

'This is my own fault,' I fretted. 'He has sensed it. He knows I'm holding back, he knows I'm not the mother I could be.'

I'd had no sleep, I wasn't thinking rationally, and I was reaching the end of my tether. In naïve desperation I even rang my mum for help.

She tutted and said: 'You made your bed, you can lie in it.'

And then she hung up. Her venom was no less than I should have expected but it left me feeling desolate. I felt as though I was under immense pressure. We were jammed in a tiny room at the hostel, with a bed, a cot, a pram and furniture all crammed in. And as I looked around me, helplessly, I felt as though the walls were closing in on me too. I could barely breathe. Ben screamed all of the time, he screamed all night and most of the day. I longed to close my eyes, just for a moment, to rest. But on the rare occasions that he did sleep I found myself wired and anxious and my head too full of neuroses to sleep myself. I became more frustrated, more exhausted, more isolated.

One day, nothing at all seemed to comfort him. He was screaming so loudly my ears were ringing and my head was pounding. I tried him with a dummy as he lay in the cot, but he just picked it up in his chubby little fingers and threw it back at me. I tried a bottle, I offered him a rusk, I gave him his favourite blue blanket, but nothing worked.

'Please, Ben,' I said, stress oozing from every pore. 'Just to go sleep.'

As I leaned over the cot, watching his angry little face, screwed up and bright red, I realised he was screaming *at me*. He hated me. Just like everyone else. Furiously, desperately, tragically, I slapped him on the face. And in the next moment the room seemed to pixellate and fall to pieces around me.

'What have I done?' I wailed.

My whole body sagged with the shame and the failure, and I was engulfed with feelings of despair and self-loathing. I locked myself in my room, and though I could hear the hostel staff talking through door, their words made no sense.

'Please, Maureen, unlock the door and let us help you,' they said.

But I was beyond help. I knew that. Wearily, I opened the door and carried Ben outside.

'Take it before I kill it,' I said, handing him over.

I told them exactly what I had done, before slumping back in my room, alone. I had failed the only living person I cared about. All I had wanted was to be a good mother, unlike my own. All I had wanted was for my children to love me, and me them. And yet I had ruined everything. Ben was taken away by social workers and I was not there to see it. I was not fit to stand there and call myself a parent. That night, after staring at Ben's empty cot, I tried to hang myself in my room, looping my belt over a hot water pipe on the ceiling. But as I stepped off the end of the bed, with the belt around my neck, it snapped and I fell to the floor in a pathetic heap.

'Typical,' I seethed, grabbing the belt and throwing it against the wall. I felt nothing but disappointment and disgust. I had tried to kill myself, yet I couldn't even get that right. I was no good to anyone and certainly not to my own son. No, I was a danger to him. That night the staff took the locks off my door and would check on me every two hours, to make sure I wasn't trying to kill myself. Ben had been taken into temporary foster care, aged eleven months.

'You can still see him,' the staff told me. 'This isn't the end, you mustn't give up.'

But I didn't believe them. My baby had been on loan, after all. I had lost him, but not in the way I had imagined. What did God have against me, I wondered, taking away two sons, one after another? It broke my poor heart all over again when I lost Ben. I had thought I could never feel pain like it after Christopher died. But this came close. Ben was not dead, but he was gone. Yet I understood that I was not the best person to look after him. I could not trust myself to be a good mother. If the social workers had offered him back to me, I would have refused. He deserved so much better than me. Again, as with Christopher, I had to think of what was best for him, and not for me. Two days on, I was arrested on suspicion of assault.

'Yes, I did it, I slapped my own baby,' I told the officers. 'I want you to charge me and I want to go to jail.'

Back at the hostel I was still on two-hourly checks. I stopped eating, not as any kind of protest, but simply because I had no appetite. I had no desire and no reason to look after myself. I had weighed around nine stone when Ben was born but my weight dropped to a little over six.

'You have to eat,' the staff urged. 'You have to get better.'

They even made me eat my meals in the office, with them, so that they could keep an eye on me. They did their best and, again, I wish I'd had the maturity to thank them. But I did not. I later heard that the charges against me were being dropped, because of my mental state. I was angry. I wanted to be punished for hitting my son. I wanted to be vilified. If life was a ladder, I was at the very bottom.

In the months after losing Ben, my life unravelled. I moved out of the hostel, with no idea of where to go next. I had no emotional structure to my life, and so I suppose this decision was a rejection of a physical routine too. I didn't want well-meaning welfare workers sticking their nose into my messed-up life and trying to help me.

I was close to giving up on myself and I wanted them to admit defeat too. I had no job and no plans, and I was doped up on so much medication I could barely string a sentence together. I was also drinking heavily. Those first few days, I stayed with an old school friend who had a flat share and a spare couch.

'Only for a few days,' she warned. 'The landlord will be on my back if you stay too long.'

From there, I went to another mate, and then another. I slept on sofas and floors. I had no idea where I would sleep or what I would do from one day to the next. During the day I walked around the town centre, aimlessly and endlessly, retracing my steps, mile after mile. I spent hours in the dole office, waiting in queues, applying for jobs, filling out forms. It all meant nothing. There was a monotony and a dullness to my days, juxtaposed with a deep hurt and a longing to see my little boy again.

'I'm sorry, Ben,' I whispered. 'Please don't give up on me. I haven't given up on you.'

I walked so far that one of my trainers split, and I could feel the damp around my toes where the puddles were seeping in. But it didn't bother me enough to buy new trainers or even tape up the hole. I just kept on walking, hoping to clear my mind of everything in it. The days were a blur and the nights were often tortuous. I slept rough more than once, and, as I bedded down on the pavement, I remembered the night I'd slept in the school boiler room as a little girl, desperate to escape the horrors at home. The problem now was that I was on the run from the horrors in my mind. But now, as then, sleeping outside held little threat for me. Unsurprisingly, I had no real friends and I was surrounded by people who were drowning in their own problems, just as I was in mine.

As I spiralled, I considered drugs as a way out more than once, but I never went beyond smoking the odd spliff. Somehow, in the fog of my reality, I managed to say no. It just wasn't my thing. I was a target for dealers and pimps, but again, I stood firm. Hidden underneath all the hurt was the spark of a survivor, still flickering. I have a hazy memory, late one night, of a bloke who became aggressive towards me, but I kneed him in the nuts and gave him a piece of my mind.

'You picked on the wrong girl,' I yelled.

I even managed to see the funny side as he swore and limped away. After what I had been through, nobody scared me. I could stand up to a total stranger, yet I could not stand up to my own parents. My mother terrified me more than any of the escaped criminals and addicts I might find myself sharing a park bench with. And though I was able to recognise, and agonise over, the dichotomy, I could not change it.

I had no contact at all with my family during these months, but they lurked at the back of my mind, like a malignancy. I never felt completely free of them. I didn't see Ben at all for five months, yet he and Christopher were all I thought about. I counted every day. I kept in touch with Ben's social worker, but I knew, without her telling me, that I was not yet well enough to resume contact with him. I had to get off my medication to get my son back. But it was not easy. I was taking stuff to wake me up and stuff to make me sleep, all washed down with half a bottle of vodka a day. My weight went down to five and a half stone and, at 5 foot 7, I was virtually skeletal. I didn't look well and I certainly didn't feel well either. I was in no fit state at all to see my son. Yet if I carried on along this path I knew I would never see him again. Deep down, the strength that had carried me through the rapes, that had seen me rise above my mother's abuse and helped me cope with the loss of my son, came to bear once again. One day, early in 1990, I woke up and decided that enough was enough. I took my entire stock of tablets and flushed the lot down the loo. I felt a small sense of triumph as I watched the tablets fizz and dissolve in the water.

'Mummy's coming back, Ben,' I said softly.

My doctor went mad when I saw him later that week, telling me I could have given myself a heart attack with such rash behaviour.

'You should have reduced the dose slowly,' he admonished.

But I had never been one to do anything by halves. And I knew this was the only way. The days that followed were hard, but I had found a new determination and I was sticking to it. Now lucid and sober, I applied to see Ben.

A Family Secret

I was told the first visit would need to be under supervision, which I understood. It was arranged that I could move back to the hostel until I found somewhere more permanent and my social worker agreed to bring him there, along with his foster mother. I was a bundle of nerves and excitement. The hours dragged until he was due to arrive. That first visit lifted and broke my heart, all at once. I felt like he had saved me and destroyed me, just with his chubby little smile. He was a little wary at first – there was a flicker of recognition in his face, but I could tell he had forgotten me. It was understandable, I told myself, it had been a long time, longer for a little boy like him.

'Hello darling,' I smiled.

I held out my arms and he reached towards me, and I felt my soul sing. My boy, he was back in my arms, back in my life. I had been determined not to cry, so as not to upset him, but I found my cheeks were wet and I did not know why.

'My, you've grown,' I told him.

He happily sat on my knee as we chatted, but then he turned to his foster mum, and said: 'Mummy, a drink!'

It cut through me and I felt my guts tighten. But again, I reminded myself, she had been a mother to him, and I had not. I had to earn the title, and right now I did not deserve it. It was a short visit, and when it came to an end I had to swallow back more tears. I knew this would take time. I knew I had to do it at Ben's pace. This time, I had to get everything right.

'Maybe next time you'd like to visit Ben at home, with his foster parents?' suggested the social worker.

I nodded, but in reality the idea frightened the life out of me. We made an arrangement for the following week, and I was torn between wanting to see Ben again and dreading seeing his foster parents. I hadn't taken much notice of his foster mother at the first visit, my focus had been solely on Ben, but now I worried that she would judge me and disapprove of me, and that I would not measure up, in Ben's eyes or in theirs.

'What will I wear? What should I say?' I fretted.

I took a little blue blanket with me, which Ben had always loved as a small baby. It had quite a large label, and he had a fondness for labels of any kind. He would often sleep with a label rubbing against his cheek, as a comfort. I rang the doorbell and stood back, with my stomach churning. I felt like I was going for the world's most important job interview.

'Come in, come in,' beamed the foster mum, showing me inside.

Hers was not the stiff, grand house I had envisaged. It was a normal, friendly, messy family home, with four other children, and lots of colour and noise and laughter. I felt instantly at ease.

'Ben!' she called. 'Mummy Maureen is here! Come and say hello!'

To my delight, he came tearing into the living room and flung himself at me for a hug. I was choked with emotion. He remembered me well from the previous week and he took the blanket from me as though he had been waiting for it. To my amazement, he took the label between his finger and thumb and rubbed it against his cheek. It was as much a comfort for me as it was for him, and I found I could not stop smiling. His foster mother was wonderful, supportive and caring, and I felt so lucky that she had helped him when I could not.

Coming away this time was very hard. I hated leaving him behind. Ben waved at the window, shouting: 'Mummy Maureen! Mummy Maureen!'

I waved and waved until I could see him no more, and I let the tears fall. But I had lots of hope too. I'd had a glimpse of what might be possible, of what the future might hold. I wanted a house like that, I wanted my boy back. And I knew I could do it. From then, my visits became my only focus in life. My social worker had initially been quite offhand with me. It was as though she'd had her fill of young girls having babies and relying on the state to clear up their mess. She didn't think I would last the course, I could sense it. But over time she softened towards me; she realised I was serious.

'You're ready for unsupervised visits, Maureen,' she told me. 'Well done.'

I punched the air in celebration. I was moving forwards, without a doubt. Sadly, Ben's first foster mother had become ill and he had to move to a new placement. I felt guilty that he was going through more upheaval, more upset in his little life, because of me. Before, I might have used this as a reason to slump back into a depression. Now, I used it as a catalyst to get better. This was more motivation to get him home with me, where he belonged.

For the unsupervised visits I needed a place where I could take Ben, and one of my sisters, who was by now married with her own family, offered to let me take him there. I needed an address to give to social services, as part of my bargain, and I was eternally grateful. This was my hour of need, and she was there for me. Seeing her, with her house, her children and her little garden, made me so envious, but it gave me something to strive for. It was what I wanted, and it was what Ben deserved. As I watched him playing with his young cousins, I made a silent promise to him that this time I was going to prove myself as a mother. And I would never ever let him down again.

Chapter 10

Just before my nineteenth birthday, social services had insisted that I started counselling sessions. After the previous abortive attempt I really didn't want to go, but I accepted it was a piece of the jigsaw, another tick on the list that was required to get my son back. But when the day came around, I felt a flash of annoyance. What could these people do to help me? They knew nothing about me. Nothing.

'It's a waste of my time and theirs,' I grumbled.

For my first session I arrived, disgruntled and plastered in makeup, in a barely there mini skirt and six-inch red stilettos. I marched right up to the reception desk and said:

'I am here to see someone called Mary.'

A few minutes later, a lady appeared and introduced herself as Mary Johnson, my counsellor. She was in her early forties and was quite petite, with a shoulder-length dark-brown bob. She wore a pale blue, buttoned-down summer dress, with a floral scarf tied around her neck.

'Oh, she will never understand me,' I groaned inwardly. 'This is worse than I even imagined.'

She looked and seemed friendly enough as she led me into a small room. But I didn't trust her at all. To me, she seemed old and out of touch. And she seemed like a snob, too; someone from a different class and a different world. Someone who would have no idea of what I had been through and how to help me. I looked at the 'No Smoking' sign on the wall, lit a cigarette and said: 'If you think I am fucking talking to you, think again. I'm here because I fucking have to be.'

I was being obnoxious, and I knew it. Rather unsubtly, I was trying to let her know that I was a lost cause. Mary said nothing. She didn't even raise an eyebrow at my colourful language and she didn't flinch as I blew smoke around the room. We spent the rest of the hour in total silence, me smoking and sighing and her simply sitting quietly. At the end of it, I realised it had probably been more uncomfortable for me than her. For the next year, that was our routine.

Every Tuesday evening I turned up for my appointment, without fail. I sat in her office and smoked, and never said a word. One problem was that I was an ignorant, immature teenager who thought I knew better than she did. But the other issue was that I physically could not have found the words even if I had wanted to. I just didn't know where to start. The shame of the abuse had left me dumb. Literally dumb. Even so, for reasons I did not understand, I never missed a single session. I could not say I looked forward to them, but neither did I dread them. Though I never spoke, I was clearly getting something out of them. Mary was like no one else I had ever met. She put up with my arrogance, my hostility, my downright rudeness without a single complaint. No matter how hard I tried to rile her, she simply didn't take the bait.

She later said to me: 'I could see the wall, and every week a little bit crumbled. I knew I could help you if I was patient.'

She had such extraordinary vision and tolerance. She could see my defences coming down, even before I could. One year on, I took her a poem I had written, about my childhood. In it were references to the abuse I had suffered, though there were no names and no direct allegations. I refused to discuss the poem with Mary, but I let her read it, and it was a huge breakthrough. The following week I took more poems, entitled: 'What are families for?', 'What, Where, Why and When', 'My Tears', 'What is Love?' and 'Why?'. Each poem was an outpouring of my distress. Then, in a whisper, as I clutched my poems in my hands, I told Mary that I had been raped, but I could not say who by.

'We'll take it at your pace,' she told me simply. 'Let's not push anything.'

Slowly, week by week, I started to tell her about the abuse by John Wood. I told her about the rapes in my bedroom and about the time he had said: 'You are my wife.' He was not a blood relative and so it was easier, somehow, to focus on him. In my mind, I wanted him to shoulder all the blame. I wanted him to be the ring-leader. I didn't mention Jock or my mother. It would be a long time before I could even acknowledge the abuse by my mother. Yet despite the violence of the rapes, my mum's abuse felt like the worst betrayal and the worst taboo. And try as I might, I could not convince myself otherwise. So, I concentrated instead on telling Mary about John Wood. Hour by hour, I shared the pain, agony and shame. By the end of my counselling I had told her more than I had ever told anyone before.

'Are you sure there's nothing else?' she asked gently.

I shook my head. I wanted to forget it. I wanted it gone. I think she knew, as I did, that the worst was yet to come. But right now I could not contemplate it. And I was still insistent that I could not go to the police. I couldn't take it any further, not yet, at any rate. What I had achieved so far, with Mary, felt cataclysmic. I felt as though I had run a marathon and I needed to get my breath back, and repair my limbs, before I ran again. And the more I compartmentalised the different abusers, the more I managed to blot out the other two. But over the years, just a whiff of old Spice, Charlie perfume and stale beer and I would be gripped by a panic attack, unable to speak or breathe. I was whirled back, like a leaf on the wind, to that bedroom with the flowery curtains and the small TV. I had to get a grip on those situations.

A Family Secret

I had to avoid all triggers as much as I could. I wanted my son back; that was more important to me than justice or closure. And so, as time wore on, I buried the abuse deeper and deeper. If I wanted to be a good mother, and a sane mother, I had to lock it in a box and throw away the key. The only way I saw a future, with Ben, was by blocking out the past completely. And so that is what I did. I dug so deep into my own consciousness that I managed to cut out the abuse totally. It was almost as though I had amputated a part of my memory.

I stopped drinking too and became completely tee-total. My friends all laughed and said: 'You will never last.'

But I was serious about this. Serious about moving on. I applied for custody of Ben, a process that would take eighteen months to complete. And from that day, I never touched alcohol. I didn't take medication. I never looked back.

Keen to prove myself to social services, I left the hostel and found a rented room in a house, shared with four or five other young adults. As the weeks went on I became friendly with another resident, Steve. For a long time we were just pals; he was going through a divorce and I had my custody application weighing on me, so we gave each other a shoulder to cry on. We each had our problems.

'We'll get through this, together,' he told me.

In the evenings we'd watch TV in his room. At week-ends we'd go for drives in his car, out into the countryside.

Steve worked at a pottery factory and was a gentle, quiet sort of bloke. I found him really easy to be with. One night, as we watched a film, half asleep in his room, Steve said: 'Do you want to come to the pictures with me?'

'What? On a date?' I asked.

Why would anyone want to take me out? Why would anyone fancy me? I was completely taken aback.

'Of course on a date,' he grinned. 'I really like you.'

'OK,' I stuttered. 'If you like.'

It had never occurred to me that we would be anything more than friends, but I went along with it because, I suppose, I was grateful and flattered.

We got on well, and I couldn't see a reason why we shouldn't take it further. Again, as with Dave, there was no spark there. I was not in love. But I doubted whether it would ever happen for me, whether I would ever feel the flush of romance I'd heard my friends mooning over. That first night out went well, and four months on I found I was pregnant. Steve was over the moon, but I was torn in two. My first thought was for Ben. My little boy. How would this affect my application? I went immediately to see my social worker, with my stomach churned up with anxiety.

'I'm pregnant,' I told her. 'I'm only a matter of weeks, it's early days, but I wanted to ask if this will go against me in my custody application? Because if it does, I will have a termination. That's how serious I am about getting Ben back.'

A Family Secret

The social worker's jaw dropped.

'I mean it,' I insisted. 'I have to think of Ben. I have to learn from the past.'

An abortion would have ripped me into pieces. I would never normally have considered the possibility. It wasn't that I didn't want this baby, not at all. But I knew that Ben had to be my priority. I had let him down and I had to rectify my failings. I owed him. If that meant terminating this pregnancy, I would do it. I had made the fatal mistake before of allowing my bond with one child to colour my relationship with the next – and it had ended with Ben going into foster care. I could not let that happen again.

'Really, there is no need to think like that,' the social worker assured me. 'Another baby won't stop you having Ben back. In fact, a little brother or sister might be nice for him.'

Her words washed over me in a wave of relief. I could have wept with gratitude.

'But what you do need is a house,' she continued. 'You need a home for your babies.'

I knew she was right. I couldn't bring up two children in a rented room. But I found myself stuck in the middle of a mass of bureaucratic red tape. When I applied for a tenancy, the council told me I could not have a house because I didn't have a child. And social services told me I could not have my child back without first having a house. It was a ridiculous situation and one that would drive me mad, over the months, making endless phone calls, sitting in endless offices, pleading my case, again and again. Steve and I were still very much together and happy, but I wanted to do this on my own. I had to show I could cope – I had to prove myself.

'I need the house,' I insisted. 'You're holding me back. You're holding my son back.'

I felt like I was banging my head against a brick wall. But I was determined not to give up. And my visits with Ben spurred me on. Thinking of his little face, upturned towards mine, lifted my spirits. Mary was a wonderful crutch too. She and I had kept in touch after the counselling finished, and I would often meet up with her at our local Christian fellowship.

'I'm proud of you, Maureen,' she said. 'I really am.'

Nobody had ever been proud of me before, and I was bowled over by her words. I found myself choking back tears and blushing at my own fragility. It was early days, but I felt so positive, as though everything was coming together, at last.

The first few months of my third pregnancy proved to be very difficult, and when a scan showed I was carrying a girl, I rolled my eyes.

'Typical,' I smiled. 'This baby is going to be hard work, just like her mother.'

I had sailed through my pregnancies with my sons, without a single hitch. But this time I felt so unwell all the way through. I had recurring kidney infections and I was in and out of hospital. I was drained of energy and nauseous all day. My visits to see Ben were the highlight of my week. By now I was allowed to take him out for the day, and we would go to the park or the museum or, if I had enough money, I'd take him out for tea. When I knocked on the door of his new foster home, I could hear his little voice shouting: 'Mummy Maureen,' and he would throw his arms around me before I'd even got into the house. I loved the feel of his hand in mine, his soft cheek against my face. I tried to push away the memories of how I had hurt him. I had to look to the future. And some things – many things – were best left in the past.

At the end of our visit, it was always so painful taking him back, and Ben never wanted to leave me either. He would often cry when we said goodbye. I kept on telling him that one day soon we'd be together for good, but I wasn't sure he understood. And though I hated to see him upset, a small part of me was encouraged that he clearly liked me. Perhaps, after all, I was not the hopeless mother I had painted myself out to be.

The day my offer of a tenancy arrived from the council, I yelled out in celebration.

'At last!' I beamed.

On 6 August 1993, aged twenty-two, I moved into my very first home, all of my own. It was the same area I'd grown up in, the same place I'd suffered those unspeakable horrors, but I needed a house, anywhere, to get my boy back. If it was on the moon, I'd have taken it. That first day, Mary turned up with a cleaning bucket and two pairs of rubber gloves.

'Let's get this place shipshape and fit for a little family,' she smiled, handing me gloves and a bottle of bleach.

She had stepped into what I imagined, what I dreamed, must be a mother's role. She looked out for me and looked after me. She wasn't afraid to hug me, or to tell me when I was out of line. Together we scrubbed and dusted and polished until my little house was ready for the arrival of my prince.

'Don't know what I'd do without you,' I told her bashfully, as she left later that night.

One week on, Ben came home. He and I danced around the empty rooms together, our laughter echoing off the bare walls, our happiness shining out from our faces. I felt so proud, so pleased. And though Christopher was in my thoughts, and always would be, I felt almost complete, too. The house had barely any furniture, but that didn't matter at all. Mary had rallied round and found me a single bed for Ben, a second-hand sofa and a microwave. Our first night, I slept on the sofa, with Ben in his little bed. I kept on slipping down between the cushions, but it didn't matter. I felt like I was sleeping in a five-star hotel. My boy was upstairs, I had my own home, with my own front door keys. It was exhilarating; both the here and now, and the promise of what was to come.

Steve had stayed on at the rented house, at my insistence.

'Just for now,' I told him. 'I want to do this properly, for Ben, and it has to be me and him.'

A Family Secret

My Ben had been through so much, for a four-year-old, and I wanted to make this transition as easy and as secure as I could for him. I wanted a few weeks with him on my own. And Steve understood completely. He was so fond of Ben. In the days that followed, Mary managed to find me a brand-new cooker from a charity contact she had. She asked around at church and even found a gas fitter to install it for free! She helped me to apply for a grant, too, and I was able to buy carpets and more furniture. I also bought clothes for Ben, and some books and toys.

Settling into family life was rewarding and nerve-racking in equal measure. I loved taking Ben to the shops, I loved washing his hair, folding his clothes, reading him stories. They were simple things. But I treasured and valued those moments so much. That September, Ben started school.

It's a proud day for all parents, but for me it felt almost surreal. I felt as though I had won the lottery. I didn't know where all this good luck, this happiness, was coming from. He settled in well, but the long days in the classroom left him starving and shattered. He would be so hungry when I collected him at the school gates that I had to have a meal waiting for him at home. Watching him sit down at the table, his little legs swinging, as he chattered away about his day at school, was a lovely time for me. Then, without warning, his little head would loll forward and he had fallen asleep, halfway through his tea! School had exhausted him to the point where he actually dozed off whilst eating. Once or twice he even face-planted into his Bolognese or his shepherd's pie! I loved scooping him up, fast asleep, wiping the mashed potato off his cheeks, and tucking him into bed. They were precious times.

'My boy,' I said proudly, as I watched him sleeping.

But I was anxious, too, about getting it right. If we were late for school, or if Ben fell over, or he picked up a cold, I worried that he might be taken away again. At first I didn't let him take risks, and of course that is what childhood is all about.

'Not the climbing frame,' I told him. 'That's too high. Stick to the swings, where Mummy can push you.'

I strived to be perfect, and like all mothers I was far from it. The weeks wore on and, inevitably, I relaxed. I learned to enjoy motherhood more and more. I learned to let myself go. One day, Ben came home from school with muddy shorts and his face was tear-stained and creased with concern.

'Whatever is the matter?' I asked him.

'I'm sorry I got muddy,' he told me. 'I know it's naughty.'

It stumped me. How could a little boy ever think that getting dirty was wrong?

'Little boys are supposed to be full of muck,' I told him cheerfully. 'Don't you worry.'

But deep down it broke my heart what he must have been through – what I had let him go through – for him to think that a few mud stains were worthy of punishment. I made a point after that of taking him out in the rain and encouraging – insisting even – that he splash in puddles, run through mud and collect sticks and pebbles.

'It's all part of being a boy,' I smiled.

And just as I was growing into the role of being a mum, I could see that he, too, was warming to his role as a little lad. In December 1993 I went into labour, six weeks early. I started bleeding at home and, in panic, I called an ambulance from a neighbour's phone. Steve was at work but he raced to the hospital and met me there. We were both concerned.

'It's far too early,' I fretted.

I was in hospital for two worrying days before the contractions began properly. Steve held my hand as our daughter, Naomi, came into the world, at 6.30 a.m. on 13 December 1993, weighing 6lb 3oz.

As she was laid on my chest, and her face turned towards mine, it took my breath away. She looked so much like Christopher. She had the same fair hair and round face. It was as though he had sent a double, to comfort me. He wanted to be a part of our new start. Despite being six weeks premature, Naomi was healthy and absolutely perfect, and I felt blessed. She spent ten days in hospital with jaundice, which the midwives explained was not uncommon at all, and then she was allowed home. Steve moved in with us and I was so happy with my little family. I kept myself busy looking after my children. Every day I looked forward and outward. But I never once dared to look in, at myself. I didn't trust what might happen. Every week or so I would change our furniture around, moving the TV to the other side of the room, swapping the couch with the dining table.

'What do you think of this?' I asked Steve, as I pulled the couch from one end of the room to the other.

He was completely bemused. He didn't understand my constant need to switch things around. I did the same in the bedrooms, too. I was always itching for change. I also did it with my own appearance; I dyed my hair a different colour every couple of months and I lost and gained dramatic amounts of weight. Back then, I thought I was just being picky, but I would learn later, much later, that my behaviour was typical of someone who had been abused.

Somehow, word got back to Mum that I had a new home and a new baby, and she turned up at the door, uninvited and unexpected. My stomach flipped when I saw her outline, dumpy and severe, through the glass in the front door. Not wanting a confrontation, I opened the door and let her inside.

'I heard you'd had a baby girl,' she said, marching straight past me.

I couldn't think of anything to say to stop her. It struck me again that I could defend myself on the streets against drug addicts and pimps, but I could not speak my mind to my mother. She had a poisonous hold over me, a vice-like control, which I could not shake. John Wood was lurking behind her, and they went into the living room and looked around, making a fuss of Ben and Naomi, as though it was the most natural thing in the world.

'Give us a guided tour, then,' Mum said.

Feeling like I was in a parallel universe, I showed her round the bedrooms. Ben couldn't wait to show off his own room.

'I'm your Nanna,' she told him with a big smile.

She was so amiable, so animated, that it scared me. I just couldn't win. Whatever side she showed, friend or fiend, I was frightened.

'We're planning on decorating, when we've saved up,' Steve told her. 'We'd like to do the kids' rooms first.'

'Let me know when you've got the wallpaper, I'll come round and help,' Mum said. 'I'm a dab hand.'

I was astounded. It was at once comforting and totally bizarre. I wanted so much to have a family, to be included in a nucleus of support and warmth. Yet this was so absolutely wrong.

'That would be great,' I heard myself say. 'I'll buy the wallpaper as soon as I can.'

I refused to think about the abuse. In fact, it was more than just putting something out of my mind. I had buried it so deep I couldn't have dug it up again, even if I'd tried. The memories were locked away in a steel safe and I no longer had the key. I don't think it was a conscious decision. I think it was all about survival. I knew, inherently, that if those memories surfaced they would destroy me – and destroy my chances of being a mother to my children. For their sake, and for mine, I had to sever all ties with my own memory.

Jock had a family, too, by this stage. Like Mum, he turned up out of the blue when he heard about our new baby. He stood on the doorstep with his own family, carrying a card and a present, just like any older brother would.

'Come in,' I said, steadying myself against the door. 'Lovely to see you.'

I just didn't know what else to say. I thought it was the best thing for everyone to let him in. And yet, though I allowed my family back into our lives, I never for one moment left them alone with my children. And so, although I had blocked out the abuse, a small part of me must have been alert to the risk. They were in my life, but I was vigilant. Always vigilant. I'm not entirely sure I knew what I was looking out for, but I was always on my guard. One afternoon, when Steve was at work and Ben was at school, there was a knock at my door and I spotted Jock outside.

'Thought I'd call in as I was passing,' he said, striding into the house.

I nodded, confused and a little afraid, though I wasn't sure why. Naomi was asleep in her Moses basket. I walked through to the kitchen to make him a cup of tea, but I could feel the tension. Every pore in my body was crackling with fear. But why? As I flicked on the kettle, I suddenly felt Jock's breath warm against my neck, and

A Family Secret

I spun around. He pushed himself up against me, right between my legs and whispered: 'How about one for old times' sake?'

All of a sudden I was bombarded with vivid flashbacks, scorching across my brain. Suddenly I was a little girl, lying in the grass on Black Bank, with Jock looming over me. And there I was, pinned down, behind the couch, my underwear around my ankles. I could see his St Christopher medal as it swung back and forth, feel his rough skin against mine, wince at the pain down below as I was brutalised and violated, again and again. I stared at his face and, involuntarily, I kicked out at him.

'I am not that little girl. You can't do this to me,' I gasped, choking on each word.

His choice of words left me reeling, seething. It was as if it had been consensual, like it had been a fun thing between us. He acted as though we'd been out together. Jock marched out of the house without a word and I sank onto my kitchen floor, shaking so hard that my teeth were chattering.

'I am not that little girl,' I whispered, as the tears spilled down my cheeks and pooled in the grouting between the kitchen tiles.

I could see the memories, out of the corner of my mind's eye, pushing to get back in. I could hear them, angrily jostling for space, desperate to be seen and heard. With a sinking feeling, I realised Jock had known I would keep quiet, that I would never dare say anything to Steve or to anyone else. He had taken a chance, knowing he had nothing at all to lose. Supremely arrogant, he had walked into my home and turned my world inside out. He was still controlling me. Jock was still my jailor. I was imprisoned. I had told myself that I was seeing my family on my own terms, but that was rubbish. They called the shots, every time. It was not Stockholm syndrome, but it was a close relative.

'I'll never be rid of them,' I sobbed.

There were two sides to me; two conflicting, battling, paradoxical camps. I wanted a family, I wanted aunts and uncles for my kids, I wanted normality. I wanted what everyone else had. I needed an antidote to those lonely nights in the damp flat with the cheap furniture and the thin mattress, in the place I had hurt Ben. I needed a sense of belonging. Yet somewhere, buried in the pit of my soul, was a burning ball of angst.

'No,' I said out loud. 'No, I can't have this. I can't do it.'

I stood up and made myself a cup of coffee. I felt as though I was physically scooping up my entire child-hood and burning it on a bonfire. I wanted nothing left, no reminders. I buried Jock's visit along with every other noxious family memory. I was almost like a witch, casting them out. Banished.

By 3 p.m. I was calm, composed, and ready to collect my son from school. Ready to be a mother again. Christmas was just a few days away and I had saved every penny to buy Ben a Sega Mega Drive – it was the must-have toy that year. I concentrated on my children, and on my future, and everything else was dead to me. I met Ben at the school gates and all the way home we chatted about Santa and reindeer and snowmen.

'Can't wait, Mummy,' he beamed.

This was what I wanted. Security, normality, purity and love. The rest could go to hell.

In the New Year of 1994, when Naomi was six weeks old, my paternal grandfather died. Jock and I had lived with him when we were small, before going into care, and I remembered him fondly.

'I'd like to go up to Scotland to pay my respects,' I said to Steve.

He offered to drive us there, then Jock asked Steve if he could have a lift too.

'Course you can mate, loads of room,' Steve agreed.

I opened and shut my mouth again wordlessly. What could I say? I was livid that Jock had assumed, with his trademark self-importance, that he would be welcome. It was further confirmation, if any was needed, that I was completely under his control. Somehow, I sat in the car all the way to Scotland, Jock in the front seat, me in the back with my children. Together we greeted and comforted our grieving grandmother. We stood, shoulder to shoulder, brother and sister. It is mind-boggling to me now. I don't expect anyone else to understand it, because I am at a loss to do so myself.

* * *

Maureen Wood

In the build-up to Christmas 1994, Steve and I began arguing more and more. There was a tension in the house; we were often not speaking or we were sniping at each other, and I didn't like it.

'It's not good for the children,' I told him.

Over Christmas I felt it so much more acutely, and I knew that something had to give.

'I want you to leave,' I told him. 'I don't want any more trouble. I just want some peace.'

I had my children to think of, and they came first, before any man. I was not, in truth, fully committed to any relationship. I doubted, realistically, whether I would ever find a partner I could feel at ease with for the rest of my life. Steve moved out in the New Year, and afterwards me and the kids settled into a new routine. I was genuinely very happy.

Admittedly, I was guilty of enjoying my own company. I preferred being alone, as I always had. And being a mother, loved and being loved, was the best job in the world. So far, since getting Ben back, I seemed to be finding my way quite well in the world, and that brought me immense joy.

Over the summer of 1995, when Naomi was eighteen months old and Ben was six, I became friendly with a man from our street called Mick. He was the ex-partner of one of my neighbours, so though he didn't actually live on the road any more he was often around. He was larger than life, funny and irreverent, and every time I saw him he would shout a light-hearted insult.

A Family Secret

'Look at the state of you!' he would shout, as he walked past my house. 'Haven't you ever owned a hairbrush?'

I could give as good as I got. He and I got on well, and just seeing him brought a smile to my face. One afternoon, a couple of months on, one of Mick's friends knocked on my door.

'Mick wants to know if you will go out with him, on a date, like,' he said awkwardly.

I suppressed a giggle.

'What is he? A teenager?' I replied tartly. 'If he wants to ask me out he can do it himself. Where's his loud mouth now?'

Laughing, I pushed the door to. I never thought he would do it. But a few minutes later Mick stuck his head around my open door, blushing bright red, and repeated the question.

'I'll have to come now, you've put me on the spot,' I grinned.

My only condition to agreeing to a date was that I could bring my children along too!

'I'm part of a package,' I told him.

Subconsciously I was probably trying to put him off, but it didn't work out. He took us all out for the afternoon, to the local club, where there was a bouncy castle and a play area. We had a brilliant afternoon, and by the end of it the kids had fallen for him, too. Mick had children himself from a previous relationship, and he was wonderful with little ones, mine included. He was just 5 foot 3, but a bundle of fun and energy. He was not in the least bit romantic but he was kind and laid back. We rarely argued – we were best friends, above all else. He was industrious and hardworking, and always in a job of some sort. He was a Jack of all trades and could turn his hand to almost anything, but when I met him he was working as a cleaner.

Five months on, our relationship became serious. I could see a future with Mick, more so than ever before. Early in 1996, despite us using contraception, I fell pregnant. That December we had a son, Josh. Mick was over the moon, and we doted on him.

'You must send your mum a picture of our new baby,' he urged. 'She has a right to see her grandchild.'

Despite my best efforts to entomb the memories and the flashbacks of the abuse, I suffered with stress and depression and there were days when I really struggled, without knowing why. My relationship with my mum was, at best, fractured and superficial. I hadn't seen her for over a year at this point, and she didn't even know I was pregnant. That was just how she was; she would blow hot and cold; nice and nasty; normal and twisted. As always, I was at the mercy of her mood swings.

'I'm not sure about sending a card,' I said hesitantly. 'We don't get on that well.'

'Oh come on, it's just a card, and she might like to see him,' he insisted. 'A new baby brings families together.'

Mick's parents were dead, and he so wanted grandparents for his children. And of course he had no idea about what had happened to me. Nobody did. By now, Mum and John Wood were living at the Masonic Hall and working as caretakers there. They were seen as strait-laced and well-to-do. Nobody would ever have guessed the sordid secrets they shared behind their starched net curtains.

Eventually, just before Josh turned two years old, I sent Mum a card, with a recent photo of the children inside, to keep Mick happy. But I didn't hear anything back and tried not to dwell on it. Three months on, Mick was in bed one afternoon, after working nights. I was downstairs, ironing, when I saw a shadow outside, reflected in the living-room mirror. Without any doubt I knew it was my mother. I would know and fear that profile anywhere. She knocked on the door and my legs turned to jelly. Much as I put on a front of being detached and unafraid, she knew, and I knew, that I was still absolutely terrified of her.

'Can I come in?' she asked politely. 'I heard you'd had another baby.'

I stood aside without a word. She made a beeline for Josh's cot and spent several moments fussing over him and admiring him.

'Say hello to your Nanna, darling,' she cooed. 'You're a beautiful boy, you really are.'

It was an emotional scene. I could almost convince myself – I did convince myself – that she was a loving grandmother.

'Your dad doesn't know I'm here,' she confided. 'He wouldn't like it. But I'd like to visit the kids, if that's OK? I've missed them. I really have.'

It was framed as a question but we both knew it wasn't. I nodded, numbly, because I felt I had no other option. I didn't ask about the problem with John Wood either; again, that was none of my business. She arranged to return the following day, later in the afternoon, when the older children were home from school. I felt sick all day, waiting for her visit. I didn't tell the kids she was coming, in case she let them down. But sure enough, there was a tap at the door, and this time she had brought sweets for Ben and Naomi. Ben remembered her from the last visit, the year before, and his face lit up when he saw her.

'My Nanna!' he beamed, and it pulled at my heartstrings.

I wanted him to have a grandmother, but at the same time I wanted it not to be her. She spent some time with the children, she gave Josh a bottle, and played with Ben and Naomi. It could for all the world have been a happy family scene. And I reminded myself, that was just what it was. Over the weeks that followed, her visits became quite regular, and she would sometimes bring a toy or a book for the kids. They really looked forward to seeing her. Naomi would stand at the window, her nose pressed against the window, waiting for my mother to come. She loved having a Nanna, just like all her friends. For Ben she was a familiar face, a connection with his early childhood, which he welcomed. I told the children nothing about her, good or bad. I simply told them that she was my mother, that she wanted to visit us, and I let them make their own minds up. And I made sure, of course, they were never left alone with her. And, if I was honest, I liked having an extended family, too. I wanted acceptance and normality. I wanted my children to be spoiled and made a fuss of. But at what cost? Looking back now, I wonder whether my mum was trying, in her own way, to make amends, through her grandchildren. I would like to think that she was sorry. But if she was, she never said so. And it's more likely that the whole thing was just an act on her part – another inexplicable strand of a deviant mind.

Chapter 11

Mick never liked to stay in the same house for long, and every couple of years he would talk me into moving. I didn't like it; I hated the packing and the unpacking, the chaos of moving day, the squabble over bedrooms. I had the vague, unpleasant sensation that I was running away. But I didn't know who from. Our little family flourished, and as our children grew older and their personalities emerged it was a joy to watch. In each of them, but especially in Naomi, I could see a small piece of Christopher. Josh was born with a condition called congenital ptosis, which meant he had no muscle in his left eyelid and it drooped. For the first few years of his life I was back and forth from the doctors, asking them to check his eyes. But I was dismissed at first as a young mum probably over-protective and neurotic, because I had previously lost a child.

'Really, you're worrying about nothing,' they told me. 'Children tend to grow out of these things.'

But Josh also had problems with his right ear and he seemed to have lots of infections, especially in the winter months. He had surgery on his ear at just eighteen months of age. After that, the operations came thick and fast, mostly on his ear but also one surgery on his eye. In all, Josh would go on to have fourteen surgeries in the first fifteen years of his life. It felt like he had only just recovered from one ordeal when we were building up the next, and I hated to see him suffer.

His entire childhood was dominated by his poor health, but he coped remarkably well. My other children had no health issues at all; it seemed as though poor Josh had got the lot. I wrapped him in cotton wool, and worried so much about him.

Naomi was a girly-girl who loved her Barbie dolls. She was very strong-willed and determined, outspoken and blunt, and reminded me of myself in so many ways. She looked just like me, too. And just like Christopher. As she grew older, I imagined his face merged with hers. It was a both a pleasure and an acute pain to see the resemblance. When Josh was born, Naomi stamped her little feet and shouted:

'Send him back! I wanted a baby sister!'

It was the start of a simmering but loving rivalry that would last right through their lives. Ben was a sensitive boy, thoughtful and sometimes a bit of a worrier. I would always be grateful to him for giving me a second chance, and I would always feel, too, that I had some making up to do, that no matter what I did it would never be enough.

Every New Year's Eve, when he'd had a couple of drinks, Mick would propose. It became as much of a tradition as a carol concert. Each year, as we toasted the New Year in front of our Christmas tree, he would wink and say: 'Are we going to get married this year, or what?'

He was desperate for us to be married. He was a traditional man, and he wanted us to be a proper family. But much as I loved him, and was comfortable with him, I wasn't so sure. We were happy as we were, and deep down I wasn't sure marriage would change us for the better.

'No,' I told him every year, with a smile. 'Ask me again in twelve months.'

We had another son in July 1999, and with four children, and a full-time cleaning job, I had my hands full. I was busy, but blissfully happy. As usual, Mick proposed again, on New Year's Eve 1999, and this time I gave in.

'Go on,' I beamed. 'You've waited long enough.'

We'd been together seven years by now. Our wedding was booked for the following September, and we invited my parents and some family members. Jock was not invited. He hadn't kept in touch for the past few years, and I hadn't sought him out. I felt a little like I was waiting for bad news all the time, like I was holding my breath, just in case. Mum had kept up her visits to see the children, and by now John Wood was coming along with her too. He seemed to make a big effort with my children, and they reciprocated. They called him Grandad, and they loved him. Much as I hate to think that now, it is true. When they visited, early in the New Year, Mick was bursting to tell them our good news.

'We're getting married!' he announced. 'She finally caved in!'

Mum seemed thrilled.

'Let me help with the arrangements,' she said. 'Your dad will give you away, of course, Maureen. Have you thought about bridesmaids?'

I shrugged. But I went along with her suggestions. I didn't oppose or endorse the idea that John Wood would walk me down the aisle. I just went along with it. I knew my place. Mum insisted on being involved with the plans, and when I showed her the cream and burgundy convertible wedding cars we wanted, she offered to pay for one. She helped towards paying for the catering and the wedding cake too.

'Don't tell your dad,' she said quietly. 'This is our secret.'

Again, I look back and wonder whether she was trying to soothe past wounds. I will never know. Throwing me a few quid towards the sausage rolls was hardly redemptive, but then, what on earth would be a suitable penance for what she had done? No amount of money or effort could ever undo the horrors of my childhood.

'Remember,' she said, as she pressed a bundle of cash into my hand. 'Keep quiet.'

It was typical of her to saddle me with another secret to keep. That March I discovered I was pregnant – again.

We had been using contraception, as always, but it just didn't seem to work.

'I only have to stand next to you and you're pregnant,' Mick announced proudly.

A scan showed I was carrying a little girl, which we were both thrilled about, but the news heralded another difficult pregnancy. For some reason, my body did not carry girls well. I was sick and lacking in energy and seemed to pick up one infection after another. With four little ones to look after, I struggled, and perhaps it was then that the cracks between Mick and me first appeared. That August, just the day before our wedding, the council offered us a new house, with a garden. We'd never had a garden before and it was too exciting an opportunity to let pass. The moving date would have to be the week after our wedding. The timing was terrible.

'We have to take it,' I said to Mick. 'This is what we've been waiting for.'

I couldn't wait for the children to have their own garden.

'You can play football and tennis and we'll sleep out in a tent in our new garden,' I promised them. 'We'll have barbecues as well. We'll have the time of our lives.'

Mum arrived dutifully early on the morning of the wedding, to help me get the children ready. Though I battled against it, and I hated to even say it, I loved her and I wanted her there. She was my mother. Satanic, depraved and horribly, terminally sick, but she was still my mother. John Wood gave me away at Knutton Pentecostal Church, Staffordshire, on a bright, sunny September afternoon. There was a moment, outside, when it was just he and I. It was a chance – and it was his chance – to say something. But it passed and there was silence on both sides. He linked his arm in mine, and I concentrated hard on my wedding day and my future. All else was buried. Mick beamed when I reached his side and whispered:

'Here we are, at last. You look beautiful, love.'

I blushed and smiled, but in reality I was uncomfortable being the centre of attention and was glad when the official part of the ceremony was over. Mary watched as we made our vows – she was my unofficial guest of honour. It meant so much to me to have her there.

On 2 September, the day after my wedding, I went into labour, two months early. Panic-stricken, I hastily packed a bag and we rushed to hospital. The doctors managed to stop my contractions and I was eventually allowed home, just in time to oversee the move to our new house. Moving day, 8 September, was hard work and disorganised, and afterwards I breathed a sigh of relief that I could finally put my feet up and prepare for our new baby.

But that same week I was readmitted to hospital with more stomach cramps. It was serious and stressful and not at all the ideal start to married life. Two weeks on, our little girl, Michaela, was born. She was a tiny little thing, still very premature, and so delicate and sweet.

She was beautiful. And again, with a new baby in the family, I felt overwhelming joy.

'Welcome, little princess,' I smiled.

I loved being a mum. But with five children and one baby with the angels, my family was now complete. I decided to be sterilised before we could have any more surprise babies. When I broached the subject with Mick, he was furiously against it. We had our biggest argument to date.

'You're being unreasonable, Mick,' I said. 'We have a big family, we're very lucky. I think we should stop now.'

He wouldn't agree. But in the end I went ahead. I'd had no say over what happened to my body throughout my childhood and I felt I had to take control now. Mick would never understand, and I decided he just had to accept that.

After my operation, Mick lost his job and was out of work for a while. Again, it triggered rows and bad feeling. I was holding down two full-time jobs, cleaning at a hospital and at a pub. I was also doing most of the housework and childcare. More often than not, I'd come home from a long shift to find the house in a mess, and it was exhausting to have to start again.

'Mick, you could help out a bit more,' I pleaded.

'I'm doing my best,' he complained. 'Stop nagging, it's all you do.'

It was strange; we had rarely fallen out during all the years we'd been together, but getting married had been nothing but a curse. It had completely ruined our relationship. The balance of power had shifted irreversibly in the household, and our roles had changed. I wanted to go back to how things had once been, but I didn't know how. One day after work a neighbour stopped me in the street.

'It's none of my business, Maureen, but Mick has been taking your daughter to your mum's during the day,' she said. 'I thought you should know. He hasn't been looking after her himself.'

I stared at her, shocked to the core. Of course he had no idea that my parents should not have been left alone with my children, but I was horrified by the deception and I could not forgive it. Besides, I had been working hard all day and it was Mick's job to care for Michaela.

'We should look after our children, and nobody else,' I told him furiously.

Mick didn't understand my annoyance. I found out that Michaela hadn't been there for long and she hadn't been alone with them. But that gave me little comfort. And for Mick and I, it was the latest flash point of many. The next day, less than a year after our wedding, I filed for divorce.

We'd had so many wonderful times together and it felt as though our marriage had just drizzled away; fizzled out before it had really got going. But we remained friends, and that Christmas, and every one that followed, Mick and I had dinner together as a family. I never wanted the children to have to choose between us, or for him to be all alone over Christmas. I was not cut out for relationships, I accepted that now. But I did my

Maureen Wood

best to make sure that the impact on my children was softened as much as possible.

We celebrated together, and sometimes it was so easy and comfortable between us that it felt like we were still a couple.

When Mick and I split up, I struggled financially and practically. I was a single parent with five children and I had to go to work, as well as looking after them all and making sure they coped with the emotional upset of their dad leaving the house. He was a big personality and so his absence was very keenly felt.

Those first six months, especially, were tough. I'd had spots of dark depression all through my life and it reared its head again now, threatening to swallow me whole. I'd had three major relationships and they had all failed. Was there something wrong with me? And was it the same fault that had caused me to be abused? Was there something rotten running through me – something I just couldn't spot? Or was I just picking out the wrong partners, time after time? Even now, as a grown-up mother of five, I blamed myself. It was absurd, I know. But I couldn't help it.

Gradually, I came through my depression and anxiety, focusing as always on my children. I did lots of cooking, and unlike my mother I encouraged my children into the kitchen with me, giving them a wooden spoon and a bowl to experiment as they wished. There were undeniably similarities between my mum and me; we shared genes and we shared a love of cooking, but I wanted, as much as possible, to distance myself from her. Together with Ben and Naomi, I rustled up big lasagnes, hot chillies and chicken curries. We never followed recipes, we just made it up as we went along.

'It's a family effort,' I said.

We baked cakes, too, a huge cake for every birthday, and more besides. It was like group therapy for us all.

Mick and I were formally divorced in January 2005. And though I was sad for the end of a marriage, I was also relieved to be single once again. It was hard looking after the kids on my own, but it was harder trying to keep a relationship going. The children were my priority, and as we worked our way around a new routine I felt new happiness and peace. I didn't do anything socially, but that didn't bother me at all. I was used to being on my own and, in truth, no matter how many people were around me, I was always, essentially, alone.

I had been single for two and a half years when I became friendly with a woman named Josie. We had mutual friends, so I knew she was gay and was going through a rough patch with her partner. I supported her when I could; we'd have coffee together or go for long walks with my dogs. To start with, there was nothing between us but friendship, but then her relationship ended, and she began tentatively flirting with me. To my amazement, I found myself flirting back. Since the very brief dalliance with the girl from school, back when I was a teenager, I hadn't given my sexuality much consideration. I'd just imagined I could bury it, like I did everything else.

I didn't want a relationship, with anybody; I had resigned myself, quite happily, to being single for the rest of my life. But over time I grew to really like Josie. It was as though something inside me had just clicked. One day we were having a coffee at her house, and, without any planning at all, I inched closer to her and kissed her. To my amazement, she kissed me back. And afterwards she laughed and said:

'About bloody time!'

The awakening inside me that day was extraordinary. I realised I was gay and I always had been. Just admitting it to myself made me so happy. I felt comfortable in my own skin, content with who I was, complete as a person. I was a gay mum, with five wonderful children, and one beautiful angel. Right from the start, I was honest with my children. Crucially, I didn't want them to hear my news from anyone else. Early on in our relationship I gathered my children together and explained I had fallen for Josie. To my surprise, it was no big deal for them at all; they were very laid back and supportive.

'A happy mum makes for happy kids,' they told me. 'Really, it's fine with us.'

But Josh, especially, struggled with the revelation that I was moving on. He idolised his dad, and for him anyone who was not his father, male or female, just would not do.

'Your dad and I will never get back together,' I told him. 'I'm sorry, Josh, but that's a fact.'

Mick was very supportive and had Josh over to stay with him for a while, while he got used to the idea of me and Josie. And as time went on he became more open and accepting. Josie and I didn't live together but we were partners and we were gloriously happy together. I felt fulfilled. At last, I was becoming who I was supposed to be in life. The children were all doing well, and we had no real problems. There were no obvious cracks. Life was good. And maybe it was too good.

By December 2007 I was just six months into my relationship with Josie, and I had to pinch myself each day with how well it was going. We seemed to be a perfect fit for each other. And there were none of the usual niggles and insecurities that I'd had with previous partners. It was meaningful without being too serious, fun without feeling too casual. Josie understood, without taking offence, that I didn't want a live-in partner. She was neither possessive nor insecure. Similarly, she enjoyed time on her own and I respected that. I was very relaxed and carefree, looking forward to the days ahead, knowing there were no obvious challenges waiting for me.

It was a novel feeling. It was like taking in a deep breath and exhaling evenly and smoothly, leaving my lungs empty and cleansed. For the first time in my life I wasn't putting up walls, making excuses or running away from someone. Instead, subconsciously I was breaking down the walls that had both imprisoned and protected me for so long, slowly yet surely chipping away at the blocks. And in doing so, I was digging down towards the buried memories. I no longer filtered every thought, every word, like an airport scanner. In my new happy place I was letting my guard down, and the consequences, like a rock thrown into a pool, would have ripples that would wash right over my head, and leave me unable to breathe.

One night I'd invited Josie to stay over, and we'd spent the evening uneventfully, discussing our plans for Christmas and making last-minute shopping lists.

'I'll have Mick here for Christmas dinner,' I reminded her. 'Hope you don't mind.'

'Not at all,' she smiled. 'You and I can do something on Boxing Day. That's fine by me.'

That was how it was between us. It was so harmonious, so straightforward. We went to bed as usual, with no warning at all of the way my world was about to topple.

During the night I woke myself up, screaming in terror. It took me a few seconds to work out that the wailing I could hear was in fact coming from me. I was aware too of a sharp, stinging pain down below, as though someone had forced themselves on me. And then the realisation smashed me in the face. I had just been raped. It had just happened. I was nine years old and John Wood was looming over me, the sickly smell of

Old Spice on his old-man pyjamas, the stench of stale beer on his breath. I felt his scratchy beard. I saw his dead-fish eyes. I saw it all.

'Maureen, what the hell happened?'

It was Josie, shaking me, trying to jolt me out of my trance. But all I saw was John Wood. Wicked John Wood. I gripped the sheets until my knuckles were white and I was soaked with sweat.

'He raped me,' I gasped. 'He attacked me.'

'It was a dream,' Josie kept saying. 'Just a dream.'

But I knew it was so much more than that. As my breathing gradually began to get more regular, I swung my legs out of the bed to go for a glass of water. But as I stood up I felt the rawness of the rape between my legs. I was reliving the horror, physically and mentally. It took about an hour for me to become fully aware of my surroundings and to realise this was not the bedroom with the flowery curtains and the pink bedspread. There were no posters on the wall, no rosary beads on my drawers. And I was not a child. At first, I said nothing to Josie. I couldn't verbalise what I had seen. More than anything, I felt embarrassed and awkward, and tried to make light of it.

'I've obviously been watching too many scary films,' I said. 'I had a nightmare, that's all it was.'

But Josie was unsettled, I could see that.

'I'm worried about you,' she said.

I was determined to put it behind me, to lock it back in the box. And for a few days nothing happened, and I allowed myself a sigh of relief. But then, without warning, another one struck. It was the same routine, where I woke, mid-rape, screaming in terror and pain, pleading for him to stop. I was on my own this time, but my yelling woke my children, who ran into my room in the early hours in alarm.

'Mum, what's wrong?' Naomi asked. 'You sounded as though you were being murdered.'

But I was not Mum. I was a nine-year-old girl and I was being held down in my bed. I heard the slap of John Wood's belt buckle. I saw him smooth down his ginger goatee before he left my bedroom.

'I've had the snip,' he said. 'You can't get pregnant. Look it up.'

'Mum!' said Naomi again. 'What the hell is the matter?'

'Nothing,' I mumbled eventually, scrabbling to gather my senses. 'I had cheese before bed. Bad nightmare, sorry. You get yourselves back to bed.'

But after that there was no stopping them. I could not keep them out. My dreams were like gremlins, burrowing into my thoughts, turning my life upside down, threatening my happiness, my sanity, my very being. They were chaotic and sporadic, with the memories flooding out, in disordered and jumbled horror. One night I dreamed about the start of the abuse, when I was a little girl, huddled in my bed, seeking refuge in the place I was least likely to be safe.

'Don't tell anyone. I'll kill you. And remember, I've had the snip.'

A Family Secret

The words chased each other round my head, muddling together, tripping each other up, until I felt I could take no more of it. The next night, I was sixteen years old, pinned down on the staircase, with John Wood looming over me like a slimy reptile.

'You're my wife this week. You're mine.'

When I woke, my heart was hammering, and the blood was pulsing so loudly in my ears I could hardly even hear my own screams. I'd thought he was going to kill me. That was the night. I thought he would rape me until I lost consciousness and then he would kill me. I was so scared, I was shaking. I wanted to get out of bed to make a hot drink, but I was worried I might meet him on the landing. I could not bring myself back to the present, no matter how hard I tried.

'Come on, Maureen,' I said to myself. 'You can't let them beat you, not like this.'

But I was powerless to stop the nightmares. Each time I awoke I was convinced that I was back in my bedroom as a child. I saw the wallpaper and I could feel the pink bed cover between my fingers. I could smell John Wood's cheap aftershave and I could see the disgusting droplets of sweat on his forehead. The scenes were incredibly and chillingly accurate. I recognised my old pink nightie. I could see my rosary beads, lying piously, indifferently, on the bedside table, like polished raisins. I saw the posters on the wall; Abba, Blondie, The Police. It was like a video tape running in my head. Each foul, stomach-churning detail was included. Each sharp pain. Each crushing drop of despair. And much as I tried to press pause, stop, eject … I could not. After one horrible night, where I woke weeping and shaking, Josie told me she had tried to talk to me, but to her amazement I had a different, girlish voice, and my mannerisms were like that of a child.

'It was absolutely unbelievable,' she told me. 'I was talking to you, yet you didn't even seem like you. You were like a little girl. I've never seen anything like it.'

'I'm sorry,' I replied. 'I really am.'

I had no memory of it, but I could tell I had freaked her out. Much later, a counsellor would tell me this behaviour was a symptom of borderline personality disorder, and that it was my way of coping. Of surviving the abuse. I tried, in broken segments, to confide in Josie. But I found it almost impossible.

'It's not something I really talk about,' I told her eventually. 'Forget it. That's what I'm going to do.'

I wanted to pull her closer, but instead I was pushing her away. All the memories focused on John Wood at first. But one night my dream began on that hot summer's day in 1979, and, as I stood in the bathroom, I heard the door opening behind me. And then Jock was bearing down on me, his hand in my underwear. I could see him clearly; the white T-shirt, the skinny jeans, the black clumpy boots. The next night I was at Black Bank and it was so clear, it was astonishing. I felt the itchy grasses on my legs, I saw the sunlight through the long ferns, and I felt the agony and revulsion as Jock forced himself on me. I woke up, sobbing.

'Please no,' I wept. 'Make it stop.'

I didn't even know if I was referring to the rapes or to the nightmares. Everything was muddling and merging into one. I was bombarded, night after night, and it was like being battered. It got to the point where I was too afraid to sleep because of what the night would bring. I began to dread going to bed. And yet I still had to function as a mother. Michaela was only six years old and I didn't want this trauma to spill over into my children's lives. More than anything, I didn't want them to suffer. I believed they had been my subconscious motivation for burying the abuse in the first place. For it to surface now and damage them as a result would be too cruel.

'It has to stop,' I told myself.

I tried to push the nightmares away; I thought perhaps I could squash them back inside. I had always known there was a box but I did not, could not, admit to myself what was inside. Each night, before bed, I gave myself a strict lecture. I was like a schoolteacher telling off my errant subconscious. Yet it was impossible. I was exhausted, confused and afraid. I became snappy and anxious with everyone around me. I felt like I was losing control completely and I worried where it was all going to end. But try as I might, I could no longer suppress what I knew were not nightmares, but actual memories. They were coming out and blasting into my reality, whether I wanted them to or not. The lock had been smashed off, without a key. It was almost as though it had blown up, from the inside. I now recognised and accepted beyond all doubt that John Wood and Jock had sexually abused me and raped me throughout my childhood. It was not a shock. It was not a revelation. But it was a truth I would rather have ignored. I had never allowed my children to spend time alone with my parents, but I had never allowed myself to wonder why. I had blocked Jock's visit, 'one for old time's sake', out of my mind. I had chased away the flashbacks and the reminders, as though they were annoying wasps, buzzing around my consciousness.

Naomi was reaching puberty and it hit me, like a sledgehammer, just how vulnerable she was, how painfully young. I was tormented by snippets of my childhood, of images of John Wood and his foul beery breath, but I did not go any further. I could not say it out loud. The memories were like rats, clawing at the inside of my brain, trying to escape. I shoved them firmly back in their cage and shook my mind free of them. As a parent, I had always been totally confident and sure of myself, and safe in the knowledge that my own children would never suffer at all as I had. I knew abused people struggled to bond, I understood that some became abusers. Yet I knew it would never happen to me. I could break the cycle and it would not be a problem to do so.

For me, this was where it had ended. But now, with the nightmares, this was where it all started – yet again. Mum did not figure at all in my dreams or in my thoughts. The nightmares, I realised, were a form of self-sabotage. Deep down, I felt I didn't deserve happi-

A Family Secret

ness. I had found contentment with my children and with Josie, and my life had reached an equilibrium. But for me, that was not allowed.

'Get her back in the gutter, where she belongs.'

The phrase dominated my thoughts. It was my own contentment, ironically, which had been the trigger for the flashbacks. This was payback for daring to try to enjoy my life. Punishment for wanting to move on. Retribution for going through my days with a smile on my face.

Chapter 12

When the nightmares first began I was on quite amicable terms with Mum and John Wood. At weekends I would usually visit them with the children. Our conversations were always necessarily superficial, but I began to find that even the simplest exchanges were becoming unbearable for me. I could not bring myself to look at John Wood, or to walk into his house. Yet I was wary of breaking the routine, terrified that Mum would ask questions and confront me. I was in such a state, I could not even think of an excuse not to visit them.

Typically, they did not notice that I was pale and quiet, and quite obviously preoccupied. Or if they did, they didn't ask what was wrong. John Wood was never usually very friendly, and he generally stayed in the living room watching TV whilst I went into the garden with Mum and the kids. He had never been a communicative man, but as the nightmares intensified I noticed he was becoming more offhand, more withdrawn. On one visit he didn't bother coming out of the house at all. He didn't even speak to me or the children.

'What's got into him?' I asked Mum.

But she just shrugged. She wasn't interested. I wondered if he had noticed a subtle change in me. Had he after all picked up on my disquiet, had he realised that I was troubled and drawn? Perhaps then he was worried the truth might be about to burst out, and with it his dirty secret. Could he see what was coming, even before I could? It was impossible to tell whether he was withdrawing for reasons of self-preservation, or whether he was just an unpleasant and bad-tempered man who did not like me or my children.

By February 2008 the nightmares were becoming so vivid that I was able to piece together months and months of abuse. During the day I would remember more details, and there seemed to be triggers everywhere I went. I could be washing the dishes, singing happily, with the kids around me, when a brutal flashback would propel me back almost thirty years and I would be left shuddering with fear.

'I'm fine, I'm fine,' I snapped at the kids.

I cursed myself as they shrank back in alarm. I was pushing them away too, hurting the people I loved the most. The flashbacks were worst when I visited my parents. Sometimes just a grunt from John Wood was enough to instigate a flashback, and in my mind's eye I could see him raping me and hear him grunting into my hair. I had to stop visiting. I was frightened of how Mum might react, but I knew, for my own well-being, that I had to stay away. I wrote to her, explaining vaguely that I had stuff to deal with and I wasn't well.

'I'll let you know when I'm feeling better,' I wrote. 'Nothing to worry about.'

I ought to have known she would not leave it there. She had never been the sort of woman to follow orders or even polite requests. And soon afterwards she turned up at my house, demanding to be let inside for a proper explanation. Again, I insisted I was ill. Which was, of course, quite true. The stress was physically and mentally draining.

'I'll be in touch when I'm back to normal,' I said wearily. 'I need some time on my own. I can't visit you at the moment. I'm sorry.'

Perhaps she stared hard at me before she walked away. Perhaps there was a shadow of fear, of uncertainty, in her eyes. But I was too wrapped up in my own angst to notice. I could not bear to have anyone around me, and my relationship with Josie, lovely as it had been, slowly fell apart. I couldn't blame her at all; my behaviour had been bizarre.

'You need to get some help,' she told me. 'Whatever is going on, you can't deal with it on your own.'

But we remained friends and she did her best to support me. She persuaded me to see my GP, who prescribed anti-depressants, without asking me about the source of my terrors. I walked out of the surgery feeling completely desolate. I knew tablets would not help. I had tried those before, after losing Ben, and they had not worked then either. Deep inside me, my secret bubbled and festered, like a tumour waiting to burst. The pressure was immense. With no outlet for my unease, I started self-harming. In the quiet of my bedroom, late at night, I began cutting at my legs, high up on my thighs, so that the children wouldn't see. The relief was all too temporary, followed by a wave of guilt and shame. I had more nightmares; this time I remembered the scene from Christopher's funeral, where Mum had punched me as I lay in bed, crying.

'Who is the father? Which one? Which one?'

So she knew, I thought, as I awoke. Of course she knew. Again, this was not a shock to me, but it was something I had successfully dodged for years. And now it had caught up with me, as the pieces of my childhood began to come together. I mustered all my courage and wrote her a second letter. This time I told her that her husband had been abusing me, and that she must have known about it.

'Remember the funeral?' I wrote. 'I do. I remember it all.'

It was a complete departure from my usual character to confront her so directly. But by now I think I was losing my sense of self, and I felt as though I was on the edge of something. I could not admit it to myself, because it would have been too terrifying. But I knew there was no way back. After I posted the letter, I half hoped that she might retaliate. I wanted to have it out with her. I needed to see her face. I wanted answers and explanations. But I was also petrified of her reaction and I regretted my boldness. As much as I wanted her to read the letter, I also wished I had not posted it.

As it was, she did not reply. The days passed and there was nothing. Her silence felt dismissive and contemptuous. As if I didn't even merit a response. With nowhere else to download my anxiety, I lashed out more at those around me, bickering with the neighbours, barking at my children. I hated that side of me; it reminded me horribly of my own mother. That I could be like her, even in the smallest of ways, was hard to take. I sunk lower still, with the comparison.

One day in June 2008, with the children at school, I reached my lowest point. Frantically, blindly, I rifled through drawers and cupboards, gathering all the tablets I could find. I swallowed handfuls of painkillers, blood-pressure tablets and anti-depressants, believing each time I swallowed I was a step nearer to peace. There was no planning, no rational thought, but I truly believed, in that moment, that my children would be better off without me. That I was so badly injured, as a person, that I was beyond help and beyond hope. I took the lot, and then called my mum. She didn't pick up the phone, and in my stupor I thought that was very fitting; it felt like a final kick in the teeth. So instead, I left her a rambling voicemail.

'You didn't protect me, and I can't carry on,' I slurred sadly. 'You failed me.'

A Family Secret

I staggered out of the house and went out for a stumbling walk, ending up, somehow, at the cemetery. I was slumped on the ground, under a tree, and losing consciousness, by the time I heard Josie's voice frantically calling my name.

'Maureen! Maureen! Thank God, here she is, she's breathing …'

Apparently Mum had picked up my message, but instead of bothering to look for me herself she had simply called my children and told them I had taken an overdose. They, in turn, had contacted Josie for help. That in itself depressed me further; that Mum would land my own children, her grandchildren, with the responsibility and the worry. And I realised she didn't care about them any more than she cared about me.

My poor children must have been panic-stricken, I realised. And another wave of guilt washed over me. Josie got me to hospital and, with my stomach emptied, I was discharged the following day. But I felt no better. What frightened me most was that I might lose my children. That I might drive them away, with my own erratic and dramatic behaviour. Or equally that they might be taken away; I was, after all, a single mum with mental health issues. I was being treated for depression and I had tried to kill myself. I knew full well that I would soon run out of chances with social services. If I didn't act fast, I would regret it. That same week I called Mary and asked for more counselling.

'I can't go on like this,' I told her. 'Something has got to give. I'm going to lose my children if I don't get this under control.'

Mary agreed immediately; it was almost as if she had been expecting this, as though she knew that one day, inevitably and irreversibly, the truth would come out. As a friend, Mary could not counsel me professionally. But she arranged instead for me to see a woman called Louise at SAIVE, a counselling service; Sexual Abuse and Incest Victims Emerge.

'This is the turning point now,' Mary told me. 'It won't get any worse.'

My first session with Louise was arranged for 22 July 2008. It was a glorious day as I caught the bus, racked with nerves, worrying how I would be able to confide in someone new. I trusted Mary's judgement, but I knew it would be tough to open up to a stranger. Louise was small and blonde, and as she came to greet me I felt instantly at ease with her.

That first meeting was in complete contrast to my first encounter with Mary, as a rude and gobby teenager. This time I sat down and told Louise everything that I could remember about Jock and John Wood and their horrific treatment of me. I was like a ball of wool, unravelling, slowly at first, snagging on knots. But then I rolled faster and faster, feeling lighter and lighter as I shared my burden.

'I want it to stop,' I said. 'I will do anything I can to make it stop.'

A Family Secret

It was like a drain bursting, and all the filthy flood-water splurging out. At the end of the session Louise looked at me and said: 'So, what do you want to do about this?'

I was stunned to hear my own reply: 'I think I should go to the police.'

Louise put her hand on my knee.

'I'll sort this out for you,' she said. 'I'll speak to the police and I'll come back to you.'

I had complete trust in her. But all that week I was a wreck. I was shocked at the complete turnaround in my approach. I had never once considered going to the police – so why say it? It had come from nowhere. The following Tuesday, Louise gave me a number, a date and a time.

'This police officer is waiting for your call,' she said.

I stared in awe at the scrap of paper, which held the shadowy possibility of justice. Far away, on the horizons of my troubled mind, the turnaround that Mary had promised was slowly taking shape. I went home and, with a heavy heart, I spoke to Ben, now nineteen, and Naomi, now fourteen. The other children were too young, but I had to consider my eldest two. This was a conversation I had hoped to avoid, yet I saw now that I had been naïve to think that. I could never have buried it forever. I had just wanted to protect them, to save them the horror and the hate that I knew they would feel. Yet right now my plan felt about as realistic as my plan to run away to London, at fourteen, with my newborn baby. I had to stay and face the music. Both times. When it came to it, I pulled no punches and I was blunt and honest.

'I was sexually abused by your grandfather and your Uncle Jock,' I told them. 'If I go to the police there might be a court case, there might be stress. I want to ask for your opinion. If you don't want me to do it, that's fine. I can live with whatever decision you make.'

It was, of course, a massive shock for them. Like all children, they loved their grandparents and their extended family. Yet they had known also that something was wrong; they'd heard me screaming in the dead of night, they knew about the overdose. They had known I was battling an anonymous enemy – and now it had a name.

'Do what you have to do, Mum,' they said immediately. 'We will support you all the way.'

We hugged, and I wept with gratitude that even though fate had dealt me a rotten hand with my childhood family, I had been blessed with golden and wonderful children. Through the thicket of stress and sadness that had sprung up around me, they were always my priority, always my shining light. I told my younger children only that Grandad had hurt me when I was little and that he had done a bad thing, so we would no longer see him.

'Mummy loves you,' I told them. 'And that's all you need.'

Early in August I spoke with the police over the phone, my hands shaking so violently I could hardly keep hold of the handset. They arranged for me to do a video interview the following day. It was a daunting prospect, but Louise promised to come along too.

'You're not on your own,' she reminded me.

An unmarked police car arrived at my home late in the morning, and I sat on the back seat with Louise. I was trembling so much that she had to hold my hand to calm me down. When we arrived at the interview suite I was introduced to a WPC named Marie. She took me into a small room with a sofa and chairs and a window that looked out over a school playground. So, as I talked about my abuse, I also watched as young children came out to play. There was a poignancy and also a purpose about that. I remembered I was doing this not just for me, but for my own children, and for all children. With the sound of children laughing and playing in the background, I told Marie all about Christopher, and his short but beautiful life. I confided how I thought he must have been Jock's baby, because John Wood had had a vasectomy.

'My stepfather was always so certain that his vasectomy would not fail,' I told her. 'He and my mother had no children and so I think he was probably right.

'Also, when Jock held Christopher, it sounds silly, but I felt a connection. I felt sure that Jock was his father.'

I told her also about the rapes from John Wood that followed Christopher's passing; the punishment rape because he blamed me for his death. The barbaric rapes when Mum was in Scotland. And those regular-as-clockwork rapes, as routine, as expected and accepted as doing my homework. That was the truth of it. I told her everything. The interview lasted four hours, and by the time I got home I was ready to drop.

Aged thirty-seven, I had finally found the courage to let go of a secret which, for twenty-nine years, had festered and blistered and threatened to eat me up completely. Yet there was no sense at all of a weight being lifted. I had a feeling of release, but not of relief. I was still so frightened, as though I had been caught under the spotlights, as though I had been exposed, somehow. I *still* felt that it was my fault. And the thought of my family finding out what I had done was too daunting for me to even contemplate.

Absurdly, I felt like a sneak, like I was a grass. I had been raised never to tell tales and here I was, telling tales on my own family. Nobody said that, of course, but it gnawed away at me. It was irrational, but it was there all the same. There was a sense of shame that stuck to me like a bad smell. I had gone to the police only because it was my last option, because I knew I could not live with it any longer. I either spoke out, or I let this kill me. The choice was simple. The next few weeks were purgatory, waiting for Marie to get in touch. And when she did, it was another crushing disappointment.

'The CPS won't touch the case,' she said. 'It's so long ago and there is no hard evidence at all. We've spoken with your stepfather and your brother and they deny everything.'

A Family Secret

It was what I had expected, but it was nonetheless devastating. Later that day Marie came to my house.

'This hasn't been done before,' she said hesitantly. 'But we'd like to exhume Christopher's body. We want to see if his DNA can prove that Jock, or John Wood, is the father.'

I gasped. I had never for a minute considered that Christopher might be able to provide concrete, Boolean evidence in my favour. That he might be the star witness in this whole sorry and sordid affair. He had saved me once, when he came into the world. Could he now save me again, having left it? Marie warned that all previous applications had been refused and that the request would have to go before Theresa May, the Home Secretary.

'Will you agree to it?' she asked me.

'I don't know,' I mumbled. 'It doesn't seem right.'

I hated the thought of Christopher being disturbed. Part of me felt angry and affronted that he should be dragged into this. Yet I realised, of course, that he was a part of this. He was at the very centre of it. John Wood and Jock were both counting on me not being able to see this through, and I had to find the strength to prove them wrong. It was too late to help Christopher, but I knew he could help his younger brothers and sisters, from beyond the grave.

'*Go on, Mum, do it,*' said a soft voice in my ear. '*I want to help you. I don't mind the exhumation. I'll do whatever it takes. Nothing can hurt me now, so you have to think of yourself.*'

I knew it was him. My beloved boy, whispering to me, when I needed him.

'Let's go for it,' I said to Marie.

The application was made early in March and it niggled away in my mind, obliterating all other thoughts. Marie warned me it could be many months before we heard a reply, so I had to try to carry on with day-to-day life. Ben, by now, was working at Alton Towers. Naomi was at school getting ready for her GCSE exams. The younger ones were moaning about homework, bickering over the last biscuit in the tin, complaining about early bedtimes. On the surface, life was normal. But underneath, there was a lethal riptide, which was about to tear me in two.

Chapter 13

On 1 June 2009 Marie called me, and I held my breath, not knowing whether I wanted the application to be approved or not.

'It's good news,' she said warmly. 'We have the green light. This is a way forward.'

She explained we would need to wait for the necessary paperwork, which might take another few weeks.

'Thank you,' I said. 'I appreciate all your help.'

But when I hung up, I felt empty. And uneasy. I was beginning to feel like I didn't care whether the case went to court or not. I just wanted my baby to be left alone, in peace. Surely that was more important? I wrestled with the decision, oscillating between what was best for Christopher and what was best for my surviving children. As a mother, I was no good to them like this. And perhaps a court case, and perhaps the merest glimpse of justice, would be enough to rid me of the demons that taunted me every time I closed my eyes. Perhaps

Christopher's exhumation was the key to my survival. As it was, I was barely coping. I was still grappling with the nightmares, and I hadn't found a way to ease them or to make them stop. Perhaps this was it. Perhaps my first-born held all the answers. Yet why should Christopher suffer? He had been through so much, too much, in his brief life. I didn't want him to have to go through this. I went round and round in circles, unable to settle on a decision. In the end, I went to his grave and sat with him for hours.

'I feel as though I'll always regret it if I pull out now,' I told him. 'I do want justice, for me, for your brothers and sisters. And for you too. Can you ever forgive me, my little angel, if I agree to the exhumation?'

I sobbed and sobbed, with my head in my hands, pleading for him to reply, begging him to send me a sign. And after around three hours I felt an incredible sense of peace and tranquillity wrapping softly around me like a cloak. I had an overwhelming sense that I was doing the right thing. Sitting on the grass, under the trees, with the red sun low in the sky in the distance, I knew for certain that my Christopher was there right beside me, at my shoulder.

'*You are forgiven*,' he whispered. '*Do it, with my love*.'

That moment at the graveside was dream-like, it was almost divine. And I knew it would stay with me for the rest of my life.

* * *

A Family Secret

Later that same month, still tortured by appalling nightmares, I saw my mother at the edge of the picture. And, as John Wood violated me, she leaned across the bed towards me and began to join in with the abuse. I saw, in sharp detail, the sick pleasure on her face. I smelled the Charlie perfume. I felt the pain of her long fingernails.

'No,' I sobbed. 'Please, no.'

It was so vivid, so intense, that I woke up weeping, confused and exhausted. I was soaked in sweat; it was as though the sheets had come straight out of the washing machine. I clutched my head in my hands and wailed, as memories flooded through my mind, one grotesque image after another.

'I don't want this,' I begged. 'I can't cope with it.'

Another night, I relived grotesque scenes of her performing oral sex on me. When I woke, I was retching and gasping for breath. My heart was hammering in my chest.

'Not my mother,' I pleaded. 'Not her as well.'

One night I was trapped in a nightmare where John Wood was abusing me. Then I felt a sharp slap on my face and my mother hissed: 'That will teach you to enjoy it.'

When I woke, my face was burning with shame. What was wrong with her? And what was wrong with me that she was so wicked towards me? Mothers were supposed to nurture, protect and cherish. Yet she was the very antithesis of all that was pure and good.

My subconscious had turned on a tap, pouring acid memories into my brain. It was as repulsive as it was vivid. A large part of me wanted to ignore it, push it away again, and pretend that my mother loved me. But a deeper part of me had known this all along. One half of me wanted to scream it from the rooftops and the other half wanted to never tell a soul.

To try to make sense of it all, I wrote it down, in a long letter, addressed to my mother. I knew I would never send it, but I hoped that I might feel unburdened somehow. But writing didn't help. Not really. I had to be brave. And then Christopher's voice suddenly came to me, as clear as if he was sitting on the end of my bed.

'*You have to tell the truth, all of it,*' he persuaded. '*Do it for me, do it for all of your children. You can't live a lie any more. It's now or never, Mum.*'

I knew this evil would destroy me if I let it; if I left it. So, with my heart thudding, I called Marie to ask if I could make a further statement.

'There's something I left out,' I whispered. 'It's important.'

I called Louise, too, and she sensed on the phone that I had something momentous to tell her. She came straight round to the house, and I was bursting to share it with her. But when she arrived, the words stuck in my throat. The idea of voicing what my alien mother – my own mother – had done, disgusted me beyond words. I could not shake the belief that it reflected on me, that somehow she had tainted me with her poison.

A Family Secret

'What is it?' Louise asked gently.

Wordlessly, I thrust the letter I had written into her hands. Her face blanched as she read it.

'I'm so sorry, Maureen,' she said. 'I can understand why you buried this, I really can.'

I hung my head.

'When Mum was abusing me, I took myself out of the room,' I said quietly. 'I used to float away on my own cloud. I think these memories were buried deeper than the others. As a child, I couldn't bear to be there to witness it, so I used to escape.

'Sometimes I'd read a book across the other side of the room. Other times I'd fly right down the stairs, away from it all.'

Louise explained it was a form of disassociation. It was my way of surviving. A couple of days later I made another statement to the police, in the same little room overlooking the school playground. I watched the children playing outside and thought to myself that their mums would soon be arriving to take them home. Mothers looked after their children. They loved them and stood by them, even when, sometimes, their fathers did not. But not mine. Certainly not mine. The fact that she was a mother – my mother – made it all the more shocking.

'*You can do this*,' Christopher whispered. '*Tell them everything.*'

It took me two hours, sitting in that tiny room, to purge myself of those dark memories.

'I remember her long fingernails, scratching inside me,' I whispered. 'I remember her getting aroused when John Wood raped me.'

I wished so much that it could have been anyone except my mother. After the interview was finished, the officers told me they had already suspected my mother was involved. They had simply been waiting to see if I would confide in them.

'After we'd interviewed John Wood for the first time, your mother was waiting at the door with a face like thunder,' they told me. 'She knew full well what it was all about. She knew what was coming.'

My mother was arrested the following day but, as I had expected, she denied everything. She had told the police I was a lunatic who was in need of psychiatric help. The file was sent to the CPS, to wait alongside the others, until Christopher's exhumation could take place. Everything rested on him. There had been times, over the years, when I had tried to kid myself that she was sorry, that in some way she wanted to make amends. When my children were small, I had lied to myself that she wanted redemption, through them. I had thought she was remorseful. But this was her chance to tell the truth, it was her chance to apologise. Instead, she threw it back in my face.

Once the paperwork came through, early in July 2009, there was a series of environmental tests on the ground around the grave, testing the soil and the air quality. The legal situation was complex and we had to be sure there was no contamination. Midway through the month, my own DNA was taken at home by Marie. Then I was told the exhumation would take place on 28 July.

'Don't get your hopes up,' Marie warned me. 'The DNA samples from Christopher may not be viable. They may not be conclusive. It's twenty-five years since his death. This is a long shot and we may end up with nothing.'

I nodded. I understood. But after my experience at his grave, I felt somehow that this was going to go well. I knew there would be no problems, not from Christopher, at any rate. He would not let me down. I had depended on my son once before, for happiness. I knew I could rely on him again. I was called to a meeting to discuss the practicalities of the exhumation and, at last, it suddenly seemed dizzyingly real.

'I want to be there, please, when my son is exhumed,' I said.

The woman from the Home Office, who was overseeing the process, shook her head in alarm.

'It's not normal for a parent to be there at an exhumation,' she replied.

'This whole thing isn't normal,' I snapped. 'I have to be there, and that's that.'

He was my baby, my son, and he couldn't go through it on his own. I had to be there for him. It was the very least I could do. Louise offered to come with me for support, and I gladly agreed. I was racked with anxiety and I needed all the help I could get. The night before the exhumation I didn't sleep at all. Plagued once again by last-minute doubts and misgivings, I wept into my pillow and begged Christopher for forgiveness.

It was already sunny at 5.45 a.m. the next morning, when Louise arrived to collect me. I was ready, pacing the living room, my nerves stretched and taut. I didn't say a word on the journey there, and neither did she; it felt respectful to travel in silence. And then, as we pulled up, I saw the glare of floodlights and the white tent around my baby son's resting place. We had been given strict Home Office instructions that we were not allowed inside the cemetery. But there was no way I could stay away. He was mine, my boy.

We had been instructed to park across the road, so that we didn't draw attention to the cemetery. But I had a good view from out of the car window and I watched, appalled yet transfixed, through a gap in the cemetery railings, as the digging began. Forensic officers in white space suits waited, like Martian pallbearers, for my Christopher, my baby, to surface. And then, there he was; his tiny coffin looked almost like a toy from where I was standing.

'Mummy is sorry,' I whispered. 'I'm so sorry, Christopher.'

As his coffin was lifted into a plain grey van, I remembered the innocence in his wide blue eyes, I smelled the newness of his skin, I felt his tiny, delicate fingers curling around my thumb. And I was overwhelmed with a tsunami of loss and despair. My poor bruised heart ached and wept to see him again. Off went the van, carrying my precious cargo. Carrying my hopes, my heartbreak, and the distant promise of peace.

Christopher had saved me once, and now, twenty-five years on, I was asking him to save me again. My guardian angel was risen from the dead, bringing with him my chance of justice.

The tears streamed down my face as Louise and I got back into her car. As the van carrying Christopher's body passed along the road, the driver slowed and nodded to us.

'Please take good care of my boy,' I breathed. 'He's so precious to me.'

We followed the van part way along the A34 and I was comforted to see that they drove slowly and with respect. The van turned off to go to the city morgue, and we continued our sombre journey along the dual carriage-way. Louise drove me home and hugged me before I got out of the car. We had barely spoken all day. I wanted to thank her for being there for me, but I couldn't form the words. I couldn't think past what I had just seen. I had been so close to my son; closer than I had ever dreamed possible. And yet he was unreachable.

I walked into the house and went up to my bedroom. In that moment I was consumed with a hatred for my parents, and Jock, for putting Christopher through this.

It could have been avoided, and he could have been left to rest, if just one of them had told the truth. They were cowards, with no thought for anybody but themselves, not even the baby they had all professed to love so much. I hated myself, too, for agreeing to the exhumation. What mother would allow her baby to suffer like this? I slumped on my bed, wondering what was happening to my baby son; my baby with the wide blue eyes and the soft fair hair.

A few days later, Marie gave me a plaque from Christopher's coffin, for me to keep. It simply said his name, but it meant the world to me. I had no keepsakes, no photos of my little boy, so this was more precious than gold. Marie told me he had been buried eight feet deep, instead of the usual six feet. At the time of his burial, I remembered, there had been a raft of strikes and walkouts, including a grave-diggers' strike. This explained possibly why he had been buried deeper than was standard. It was a quirk – but it had turned out to be crucial. The soil around Stoke-on-Trent was famous for its clay, hence the pottery factories that had once domi-nated the city's economy, and my baby son had been buried along the clay line, meaning that his tiny body was perfectly preserved. The chances of a viable result were very high.

'*See*,' said a little voice. '*I told you it would be fine, Mum. I told you!*'

DNA had been taken from four areas and both his little femurs, along with two bones from his arms that had been removed. I wanted the information – I demanded it from the police. And yet I recoiled from it too. It was awful to envisage. I imagined a sharp knife cutting into my baby boy, ripping out his limbs, and I clamped my hand over my mouth in horror. My eyes swam with angry tears. All of this was their fault. John Wood. Jock. My mother. They would rather see my baby dug up and cut up than own up to their own evil. This betrayal, to me, felt like another form of abuse. Another show of control.

'*Don't let them get to you*,' Christopher reminded me. '*Don't let them break you.*'

In August the results came through. I was on tenter-hooks all day, waiting for the phone to ring. When it did, I jumped out of my skin.

'It's a perfect match,' Marie told me. 'I can't believe it.'

There was a 1.5 million-to-one chance that Jock was not Christopher's father. He was a baby from familial, related parents. I had, of course, known that all along. This was simply confirmation that I was not the liar and the lunatic my family claimed I was. Whilst I was hugely relieved that it hadn't all been for nothing, there was no celebration. No sense of joy or achievement. I could not even bring myself to smile. It seemed deeply inappropri-ate. This was a stomach-turning, soul-destroying situation. But now I knew that Christopher was helping me, it gave me the strength to see it through. He had done his bit and I would do mine. Together, we were a team. I felt like I had someone on my side, and it was nice.

'*I'm here, Mum,*' he said gently. '*Always.*'

I remembered how, after Christopher's death, my parents had argued heatedly about the final resting place for his remains. Mum had insisted on burial. John Wood had wanted a cremation. I, of course, had no say at all in the matter. I was not even consulted. But I remembered the rows.

'It's a church burial and that's final!' my mother had shouted.

'A cremation would be so much simpler,' he had argued.

At the time I hadn't realised the significance. But it occurred to me now that perhaps John Wood had wanted to hide the truth, to destroy the evidence, once and for all? Maybe he had worried that one day Christopher's body could be used to convict them. It was more likely that he had simply favoured the cheaper option, which was cremation. But Mum had got her way in the end, as she always did, and had him buried. That decision had proved to be her downfall. One way or another, the truth was going to catch her and crucify her.

My priority now was to make sure that Christopher was reburied with dignity and love. And this time, unlike at his first funeral, I would organise it all myself.

'It's not government procedure,' said the official from

the Home Office, when I told her of my intentions. 'Bereavement Management usually take care of this.'

But I shook my head.

'I'm his mother, and I will do it all,' I said firmly.

'But parents are not usually present at the reburial,' she explained. 'Just as at the exhumation.'

But I wouldn't hear a word of it. I realised I was creating a headache for the Home Office and all their red tape, but I didn't care. As a teenager, I had been pushed around and bullied for my son's first funeral. And there was no way I would let it happen again. I wanted to make amends, as much as I could. I owed him that much, at least. I had to lay his ghost to rest with the respect he deserved.

'Please leave it to me,' I begged her. 'It's something I have to do.'

I went to the funeral directors of my choice and picked out a tiny coffin. I chose the flowers and the prayers. I had never been allowed to make a single decision for my son, in life or in death. I had never even chosen a pair of bootees for him, yet here I was choosing a coffin. I paid every penny myself, too. The Home Office had of course offered to pick up the bill, but I flatly refused. It was so important for me, and for Christopher, that I did this for him.

On the day of his reburial, that August, it poured down – just as it had for the first funeral. If I closed my eyes and listened to the rain hammering on the windows, I could almost imagine I was back there, in my parents' house, waiting for the hearse, waiting for my own bleeding heart to stop beating. I could hear John Wood and Jock squabbling over who would carry his coffin. And I could feel my mother's fist as she pummelled my head in the bedroom:

'Who is the father? Which one is it?'

It was like losing my baby all over again, and the grief brought me to my knees. I hadn't slept at all the night before his funeral. And through the darkness I fancied I could hear the soft, twittery sounds he made when he was asleep.

At 9 a.m. I went to collect the blue balloons I had ordered. Next, I picked up his flowers; white roses, because white is the symbol of innocence and purity. And despite his beginnings, my Christopher was pure and unblemished. Mick arrived at 10 a.m., to look after our younger children; I thought they were too little to attend the reburial. Soon after, Mary and Louise knocked on my door, along with the pastor. And together with Ben and Naomi, we left for the cemetery. It looked very different to the last time I'd been there; today, in the grey rain, it looked so ordinary. There was only the small mound of earth, at his graveside, as a reminder. The pastor began with a few words of prayer and then I read a poem I had written myself, which I would later have tattooed onto my leg as a permanent memorial.

A Family Secret

What can I say about you today, it's so hard to find the right words to say.

You have given me so much yet left me so long ago.

You showed me what love was when you were with me,

What sorrow was when you left me.

Yet today you have achieved so much more than I would ever have dreamt of,

You have shown after all these years that you still count in this world,

You have proved that I was right in these steps that I have taken,

You have shown me that trusting in the truth will always pay in the end.

Christopher, my darling, you were born from something very wrong,

Yet you will remain so innocent and pure forever more.

Thank you form the bottom of my heart.

Thank you for helping to give me my life back.

Thank you for just being you.

Thank you for helping me to get through this.

Christopher, my angel, so fair and sweet.

Now my darling may you finally rest in peace.

Sleep tight little man and know you are never far from my thoughts.

Mary gave a reading, too. And then, in the rain, we each threw a white rose onto Christopher's coffin and released a balloon for him. At home, at the same time, my younger children were releasing balloons too. It was a simple ceremony, but it was sincere and heartfelt and exactly as I had wanted it. Everyone who mattered was there, or was at home and thinking of him. I didn't cry at all, because this was about celebrating and honouring the most remarkable of little boys. He had lived for less than a month, but he had achieved so much. He had taught me how to love in life and how to go forward after his death. I knew, fiercely, as I stood at his grave, that I owed it to him and his memory to see the case through, regardless of the outcome.

'I will do my best,' I promised him. 'I'll make you proud. I won't give up.'

'*I don't doubt it*,' he whispered, his voice pattering in the rain. '*I know you can do it.*'

By the time I got home, after the ceremony, I was ready for the biggest fight of my life.

The weeks after Christopher's reburial were hard. My sleep was still infested by nightmares and flashbacks, and I was suffering with severe exhaustion and crippling stress. There were days when I really felt I could no longer go on. Despite everyone around me reminding me I was not at fault, I blamed myself for putting my children through such worry and distress. My children, as always, were a wonderful safety net, together with

A Family Secret

Mary, Louise and Marie. And, of course, Christopher hovered at my shoulder, whispering support in my ear, pulling me back from the brink, time and time again.

'*I am with you, always*,' he told me.

I felt his presence so strongly. Sometimes I fancied he hovered above me, like a ghostly butterfly. Other times he was perched on my shoulder, like a small, wise owl. Always, he gave me strength. At the end of September I made my victim impact statement. It was emotionally draining and I decided to have a nap before the children came home from school. When I woke I had a string of missed calls from Louise and from Marie, and text messages urging me to get in touch. I called Marie, my heart thumping, knowing there was a big announcement waiting.

'The CPS have made a decision,' she said.

I felt sure the news was bad. I was convinced my family would walk away from the charges, and I would be left to cope with an almighty fallout. Nobody had ever listened to me my whole life. So why would they start now?

'They are pressing charges against all three,' Marie said.

It took a moment for the words to sink in. This was not what I had expected, not at all.

'Wow,' I gasped. 'I'm flabbergasted.'

Again, I felt no sense of victory, no joy. But I did feel a quiet sense of satisfaction, and momentum. I was finally making waves. My voice was finally being heard. John

Wood was charged with multiple rapes. My mother, with aiding and abetting rape. Jock was charged with rape, incest and indecent assault. To know that they would face reckoning and accountability for what they had done was colossal. It felt terribly sad, in a way, but above all it felt like the right thing to do. The police ordered John Wood to hand over the deeds to Christopher's grave, but he did so only after his solicitor advised him to. Marie brought the deeds for me and as I stared at Christopher's name, in black and white, I felt again that I was drowning, struggling to stay afloat in a sea of uncertainty.

'I'm really struggling,' I confessed. 'I keep thinking about the exhumation and what my son went through. I'm pleased about the charges, I think. But I'm worried about the impact on my children, Marie. I don't know if or when or even how this is going to end.'

Marie nodded understandingly.

'This is a positive course of action,' she reminded me. 'You are showing your children that no matter who hurts you, and no matter how long ago it was, you must speak up and tell the truth. That's such a valuable lesson, and it's a brave one too.

'You're doing well, Maureen. You're still standing. And that's an achievement in itself.'

They were wise words, and I knew she was right. I also knew it would be months before the case came to court and I had to stay firm. I could not afford to let myself slip or to question my resolve.

A Family Secret

'*You're still standing,*' Christopher reminded me. '*One day at a time.*'

Chapter 14

To give myself a focus, I began planning for Christmas. I put the decorations up in mid-November and started my Christmas shopping. Though I was a single mum and I was always short of money, I overspent every year on the kids. Nothing gave me greater pleasure.

'If I don't spend on you, who do I spend on?' I grinned.

One afternoon, Naomi and I went shopping into the city centre. She had nipped into Primark to choose new Christmas pyjamas for Michaela and I was waiting outside, because the crowds were unbearable. I wanted to catch my breath for a few moments. But as I gazed down the street, admiring the Christmas tree and the sparkling lights, I suddenly froze in horror. There, heading straight for me, was my mother. I went into panic, my pulse racing, my blood running icy cold. Frantically, I crouched down low, behind the brickwork of the shop façade, and tried to hide my face behind one of my shopping bags. Carefully, cautiously, I peered out – and there she was. She was just a few feet away. My heart thudded as she drew nearer. It was like waiting for an electric shock. It was all I could do to stop myself screaming. As it was, she didn't even see me. She walked straight past. I had built myself up for a huge confrontation and it had fizzled away into nothing. But just the idea of her being on the same street, just the notion that we might cross paths, was enough to reduce me to an anxious mess. I was still curled up, trembling, when Naomi came out of the shop.

'Mum, what on earth are you doing down there?' she asked.

'I saw her,' I stuttered. 'Your Nan is in town.'

Our Christmas shopping day was ruined. I knew I couldn't continue, knowing I might see her again.

'Let's get you home,' Naomi said kindly. 'We can shop another day, it's fine.'

But we still had to get back across town to the bus station. I felt hunted, peeping around each corner in case she was there. My head was swivelling like an owl, scanning like a CCTV camera. I was a bundle of nerves as we queued for our bus home, in case she turned up at the bus station.

'Calm down, Mum,' Naomi reassured me. 'You've done nothing wrong. She should be the one who is frightened of facing you, not the other way round.'

I knew Naomi was right, but I couldn't explain my fear and nor could I shake it. How the hell was I going to face my mother in court if I couldn't even walk past her in town? In court, I would be meeting my maker. Literally. And it frightened the life out of me.

Naomi celebrated her sixteenth birthday in mid-December and we had a family meal at home. I cooked up a storm and found I really enjoyed myself. I baked her a big birthday cake too. Once again, cooking gave me a sense of serenity and calm, just when I needed it most.

'Happy Birthday to you ...' we sang, and, as I watched my children's faces, glowing with happiness, I felt myself smiling too.

We had a busy, chaotic Christmas, with wrapping paper and half-eaten mince pies scattered everywhere. The house was filled with giggling and bickering and noise and life. It was just how I liked it. I managed to laugh along with the kids, enjoy the Christmas films and push all my problems to the darkest recesses of my mind. In the New Year I began to feel more positive about the future. I was scared to death about the trial, but I could also see an end in sight and, with it, some closure for my family. I knew if I could just get through it I could start to put this whole thing behind me at last.

The trial date was set for 11 May 2010, and I was both dreading it and willing it forward. To keep myself on track, I wrote reams of poetry, with my fears and feelings spilling out over the pages:

Hopeless days, endless nights, constant battles,
useless fights,
    Fretful dreams, heartfelt hopes, truths to be
told, struggles to cope,
    A victim's life, a survivor's dream, nothing's
ever as simple as it seems.
    Future seems bleak, past is worse, middle of
it all, finding new firsts;
    First time to cry without feeling fear; first
time to tell someone you hold dear;
    First time to be totally believed; first time to
feel utter relief;
    First time ever not to be judged; first time
ever down your path you must trudge;
    First time to face your childhood demon; first
time to believe you really are human;
    First time to let go of your awful past. It may
be the first, but it's also the last.

At the end of January 2010 I was taken to see the court
by a victim liaison officer.

'It's a good idea for you to look around and get used
to the place,' she advised.

But even on a trial run, in an empty court, I was
apprehensive. I had never been in a crown court in my
life. When Ben came home I'd been to the family court
to finalise the custody order, but that was nothing like
this. As we walked inside, my stomach lurched and my
mouth ran dry. The victim liaison officer kindly showed

me where the defendants would be, and also the jury, the barristers and the judge. It was intimidating and harrowing just looking around me.

'And this is where you will be,' she said, pointing to the witness box.

Special measures had been put in place so that I could have a screen to protect me. I had insisted on this, knowing that I would never be able to concentrate on my evidence with Mum's eyes boring into me.

'This is just how it will be for the trial,' the liaison officer explained, showing me a thick, dark curtain, which went from the ceiling to the floor. I sat down in the witness box to try it out, and she pulled the curtain across. Immediately, I felt muffled and suffocated. I was trapped – I was imprisoned – and it was as though they had me exactly where they wanted me. Again.

'No,' I gasped, with my blood pounding in my ears. 'I'm too closed in, I can't bear it. I don't feel like the victim, I feel like the defendant. I feel like I'm on trial here.'

I suffered a panic attack, right there in the witness box. My heart was thumping so loudly it threatened to jump right out of my chest. I sat with my head in my hands, trying to slow my breathing and stem my tears. I knew if that happened at the trial it would be game over.

'I'll have to give evidence without a screen,' I said to her. 'It's the only way.'

Of course, it was a huge decision for me. I would have

to face my abusers and my rapists, who also happened to be my mother, my brother and my stepfather.

'Are you sure?' asked the officer doubtfully.

'I can do it,' I said aloud, more to convince myself than anyone else.

Deep down, I wasn't really sure at all. Was I bold, or stupid? We walked out of the courtroom, with my legs still shaking, and I sat down on a bench. Could I really go through with this? Could I put my own parents in jail? There was a strange dichotomy in my attitude to my parents and my brother. Whilst I loathed and despised them, I also felt an irrational but palpable sense of guilt. I knew the court case would destroy them, and also my siblings, and my wider family. I had to live with that. I was the black sheep. I was the one who had thrown a rock and smashed open the glass house where my own family lived.

Time seemed to slow down and almost stop completely as the court date drew nearer. Then, with one day to go, it was delayed for a further two days because Jock's defence team said his DNA results were not ready. I was livid. He'd had months and months to get his case ready and this, I knew, was nothing more than an attempt to unsettle me and throw me off course. And to my annoyance, it worked. On the morning of the trial, I was outside the court buildings by 8.45 a.m., pacing the pavements and trying to pluck up the courage to go inside.

'*I'm with you, Mum,*' said a soft voice at my shoulder.

Knowing I was not alone, I took a deep breath and pushed through the glass doors. After security checks, I walked into the foyer – and came face to face with Jock. He was sitting on the seats outside the witness support room, for all the world like an innocent bystander. I couldn't believe it. I half thought I was hallucinating. I registered a look of surprise and alarm on his face and realised, with a jolt, that he wasn't expecting to see me either. Mumbling and sweating, I managed to find a member of the court's staff and I was shown into a waiting room and away from him. As I got my breath back, and sipped a cup of tea, I remembered the look on Jock's face. I knew that he hadn't been expecting me at all this morning. He had thought I would bail at the last minute. Throughout my entire life he had bullied and controlled me. He had presumed and assumed that I would always stay silent. And now, as the moment of reckoning approached, he was counting on me losing my nerve, as always, and letting him walk free.

'Not any more,' I said under my breath. 'No way.'

Sure enough, my barrister came to see me and said that Jock's barrister was indicating a change of plea.

'He waited to see if I was going to turn up,' I said bitterly. 'He's only pleading guilty because I'm here, because he has no other choice.'

My barrister nodded in agreement. We were called into court at 11.30 a.m. to hear Jock plead guilty to indecent assault, rape and incest. The trial was then adjourned for the CPS to prepare an updated case against my parents.

'I'm afraid that's it,' my barrister explained. 'You have another long wait ahead, until we get a new date.'

My head was swirling with a maelstrom of emotions. I was relieved that Jock had pleaded guilty but also furious that he had waited until the last possible moment to do so. The evidence that he was Christopher's father was irrefutable, but he had hoped – and believed – that I would not be brave enough to face him in court, and that my case would collapse. He had only told the truth to save his own skin, pure and simple.

'Who's the coward now, Jock?' I said to myself. 'Who's running away?'

In spite of myself, the smallest part of me felt some sympathy for Jock. He had looked white, like a broken man, when he saw me walk into the foyer. Gone was his usual arrogance and his self-confident swagger. Images flashed through my mind: Jock playing his music loud and Mum hollering up the stairs at him, Jock seeing my broken nose and going off to punish the culprit, Jock coming home from the barbers with a Mohican and sending Mum into a frenzy. He was still my big brother. I could not escape that.

I was angry at myself for being so soft. The very fact that he was my brother should have guaranteed I was safe with him, I knew that. Yet empathy and affection were not taps I could simply switch off. This conflict, this misplaced loyalty, had blighted my entire life. It was, of course, the reason why I had waited so long to fight for the truth. And now, at the last hurdle, it threatened to eclipse my chance of justice completely.

'*Hang in there, Mum,*' breathed a voice at my side. '*One guilty, two to go.*'

I was frustrated that now I faced yet another long wait, another agonising build-up before my parents could be dealt with. Everything was back on hold. And the wait for a new court date hung over me, like the gallows. For the next ten months I lived on my very frazzled nerves. I went from eighteen and a half stone to twelve stone. I seemed to burn calories away just through worrying. It was the sort of weight loss I would normally have been thrilled with. Now it served only as a harsh reminder of what was ahead. The new date was set for March 2011, and somehow I got through the days, one at a time. I celebrated my fortieth birthday in October 2010, and Mary and Louise took me out for a meal to celebrate. We had a party at home, too. But somehow it felt like the last supper.

I got through another Christmas, another round of children's birthdays, painting on a smile, baking cakes and wrapping presents. I tried hard to throw myself back into family life. But I was simply going through the motions and filling in time, like a woman destined for the electric chair. When it came around it was almost a relief, just to get it over with. Louise picked me up for the first day of the new trial. Ben and Naomi came to the court with us, and the younger kids stayed with Mick.

A Family Secret

Neither of us wanted the three younger ones to know the sordid details. I could count on Mick now even more than when we were together, and I was thankful for that. He had been shocked and outraged when I told him about the abuse, but supportive. The trial was listed to last for ten days and I was due to give evidence on the second and third days. I was warned I would be questioned by three barristers – the prosecution and one each for the defendants.

'You can have as many breaks as you like,' the witness protection staff told me.

But that was little comfort.

As I walked into the courtroom to take my seat in the witness box it was like walking from my bedroom into my parents' room, ready for the fortnightly horror of abuse. I felt my feet shuffling slightly, as they once had in my slippers, reluctant to make the short trip across the landing. It was just a few steps, but it seemed to take years. And in some ways I didn't want the walk to end. I didn't want what was coming next. Yet I could not avoid it. Suddenly I was a little girl again; helpless, afraid and alone. I did not look at the dock, I did not look up at all. But I could feel their eyes boring into me. I could smell the Charlie perfume and the Old Spice aftershave. My heart pounded against my rib cage as I remembered the flowery curtains, I saw the depraved joy on Mum's face, and heard John Wood grunting and sighing, his rancid breath damp on my ear.

'Block it out,' I told myself firmly. 'Deal with it later.'

My barrister questioned me first. Then Mum's barrister stood up to face me, and if I had been attacked by a rabid dog I could not have felt any more traumatised.

'Why are you telling lies?' he snapped.

'Why would I lie?' I stuttered. 'Why would anyone put themselves through this ordeal in a court?'

He fired questions at me, demanding to know why I hadn't reported Mum's abuse at the same time as John Wood and Jock's. He claimed my allegations were simply a figment of an over-active imagination.

'You want revenge on your parents because your brother raped you – you blame them, don't you?' he insisted.

Louise had warned me not to lose my temper, but it was so hard. I felt as though I was the one on trial, that I was the one in the wrong. She had advised me also to tell my story to just one person in the jury and concentrate on them, and nothing else.

'It will calm your nerves,' she said.

So, as the barrister ranted and raved, I focused on a man in the jury in his forties, with greying hair and a kind, gentle face. I tried to explain how the memories had surfaced piece by piece, how they had to be coaxed out of the depths of my mind, because it was otherwise too painful and too overwhelming. I told him that I truly believed I might not have survived if the whole thing had come out at once.

Mum was sat just a few feet away, and I sensed she was watching me. And pounding away in my mind the whole time was the knowledge that she could have saved me from all of this. She could have prevented the exhumation. She could have prevented the court case. Simply by telling the truth. The enormity of the betrayal, of the rejection, by the woman who had given birth to me had never been more stark or more sickening. And it had never hurt more. I had been determined not to let my guard down, but the tears came and I sobbed uncontrollably, in front of the whole court.

'We'll take a break,' the judge announced.

During the break I walked outside for some fresh air and was dismayed to see Mum there too, having a cigarette. She looked blank. Totally without emotion. I called it her 'pan face'. I had seen it so many times before. It was the same facial expression she'd worn when she battered me, at Christopher's funeral. She gave nothing away in her face. Perhaps, I reasoned, that was because there actually was nothing to give away. Perhaps she was an empty vessel. A cold, unfeeling, unmaternal mother. I went back into court, shell-shocked as much by my mother's lack of reaction as by the cross-examinations.

'Tell me again why you lie so much,' said her barrister. 'Tell me why you can't differentiate between dreams and reality.'

My evidence, punctuated by frequent breaks, lasted for hours. Afterwards, I felt totally defeated; drained and squeezed out. I wasn't at all sure I could do it all again the next day, at the mercy of John Wood's barrister.

Early the following morning I had some cereal, but threw it all back up. My stomach was churning. This was so much harder than the police interviews. The barristers in court were absolutely brutal.

'They're like professional bastards,' I said wearily. 'I feel like they really want to destroy me.'

John Wood's barrister focused on the fact that his client was an upstanding man, respected and valued within the community.

'Not within his own home,' I thought.

But I said nothing.

Again, I was accused of lying. Again, I wept tears of frustration and fury. But a little voice, just level with my shoulder, reined me back in.

'*You can do this, Mum,*' Christopher whispered. '*Remember, I've done my part. I'm with you.*'

And I knew I was not alone. I wiped my eyes, blew my nose, and carried on. By the time my evidence was finished I felt like I'd been chewed up and spat back out. I had been on the stand, in total, for ten hours. I continued going to court every day even though I was not required to. It was totally compelling and held a morbid fascination for me. I didn't want to be there, and yet I couldn't not go. But as I got to the door of the courtroom on day four, and heard John Wood's cold, measured voice, I froze. I couldn't go in.

That voice threw me right back to my childhood.

'And don't worry, I've had the snip.'

'And if you tell anyone, I will kill you.'

A Family Secret

'So, you will be my wife this week.'

I shuddered, trying to shake the memories out of my head. Instead, I went into the witness room to wait. There were only two witnesses for the defence: Him. And her. I was told that Mum had collapsed on the stand and claimed she could not breathe. The trial was halted, and an ambulance was called. But I had seen her outside earlier, smoking and staring ahead with her 'pan face'. I knew the collapse was nothing but a show for the jury. She was all about keeping up pretences and always had been. And sure enough, she was back in the dock that same afternoon, having recovered rather quickly. Jock had to be at the court, too, as he was listed to be sentenced at the end of this trial, should they be found guilty. And on the sixth day Jock's barrister asked Marie if I would be prepared to speak to him.

'As long as I'm not on my own with him,' I agreed.

Truthfully, I wanted to face him. I wanted to know why he had denied being Christopher's father for so long. We met in a small witness room, with police officers on either side.

'Have you accepted you are Christopher's father?' I asked. 'Finally?'

'I have no choice,' he replied.

'But you knew, all those years ago,' I insisted. 'Otherwise, why did you ask if you could carry the coffin at his funeral? You asked because you knew you were his father.'

Jock shook his head angrily.

'I asked because I was the man of the house and it was my place to carry him,' he said.

I knew he was lying.

'John Wood was man of the house,' I countered.

'No, he wasn't,' Jock replied, rattled. 'I was.'

He wouldn't accept responsibility. Wouldn't even look me in the eye. The silence stretched painfully between us.

'Have you nothing else to say?' I asked eventually.

'Like what?' he said.

'Well, an apology, an admission of what you did?' I said sadly.

Jock glared.

'I have nothing to apologise for,' he spat. 'I pleaded guilty. What more do you want?'

I was angry myself now.

'You should apologise to Christopher,' I said. 'He is your son and because of you he had to be exhumed, because you wouldn't admit what you did.'

But Jock still refused to say sorry. He said nothing at all.

I threw my hands up and left the room. It was almost as though he felt he had done me a favour by pleading guilty. He acted almost as though I was making a fuss about nothing, as though I was over-dramatising the entire situation. I had no idea why he had asked to see me, because he had nothing to say. I had done all the talking. I had made all the effort. Once again, he was controlling me and pulling all the strings and I was mad at myself for even agreeing to see him. Jock had had a tough life. But so had I. And nothing could ever excuse the way he had behaved.

Despite everything, I was glad I had agreed to see him. It did at least mean that I was left with no illusions. As we whiled away the long hours in the witness room, Marie and I chatted and I spoke to her about the involvement of social services in my childhood.

'When I look back, I can't believe that nobody at all noticed what I was going through,' I told her. 'I used to think that someone, somewhere, would rescue me. There were so many warning signs. Yet nothing ever happened.

'It was all the more puzzling because we'd had social workers crawling over our family like ants so much of the time. It wasn't even as if anyone needed to alert them, because they were already there. But they had never picked up on a thing.'

One afternoon, I steeled myself and began reading through my social services file – and seeing one page, my blood ran cold. There was a short note, taken from Jock's records, that someone had reported him for abusing one of his sisters. There was no name. But there it was, in black and white, that somebody knew. Given what happened to me, surely social services should have investigated?

It seemed quite incredible. I'd had an unexplained pregnancy. I'd been to hospital with urine infections and a vaginal injury, apparently from sitting on a bike. I'd run away countless times. I was deeply unhappy and disturbed. And, for the final, devastating piece of the jigsaw, Jock was known to be abusing one of his siblings. It defied belief that nothing had been done.

'It could all have been avoided,' I said bitterly. 'The whole thing.'

It was a mini hand grenade into my life. But at that moment I was dealing with an atom bomb, with the trial going on around me. Whatever shock and outrage I felt over social services would have to wait. On the tenth day the jury went out to deliberate. I paced the corridors, unable to relax, unable to focus on anything else.

'Let's go outside,' Naomi suggested. 'Let's have something to eat and try to settle your nerves.'

She and I went outside, along with Ben, to sit on a bench in the spring sunshine. Naomi's friend, Ash, had brought us a picnic, and we ate sausage rolls and drank lemonade, pretending to the world that it was just a normal day. That little splash of kindness from Ash meant so much; it was like an arm around the shoulder. As we sat and ate, Ben told me how, a couple of years earlier, John Wood had taken him aside over Christmas and said: 'No matter what you hear, no matter what people say about me, I will always love you. You will always be my grandchildren.'

'I thought nothing of it at the time,' Ben told me. 'He'd had a few glasses of red wine and I just thought he was drunk and rambling. Looking back, I think he saw this trial coming. He must have been worried you might go to the police one day and he was trying to explain himself. Not that he ever could.'

I shivered. John Wood had lost the right to be a grandfather a long time ago. The jury came back first on John Wood, and as we filed into court I prepared myself for the inevitable disappointment.

'Guilty on all charges,' said the foreman.

I felt my knees buckle as I gripped Ben and Naomi's hands on either side of me.

'We did it, angel,' I whispered. 'Me and you.'

'*Well done, Mum*,' Christopher said softly. '*I knew you could do it*.'

There was no celebration, no time for it to sink in. The jury went back out to continue deliberating Mum's guilt. John Wood was remanded into custody immediately. He asked rather pathetically if he could be allowed to go home overnight to pack up his things, but his request was refused. He'd had years to make his plans for going to jail, I thought to myself. Truth was, like Jock, he'd never expected me to take it this far. He didn't think I had the bottle.

The following day the foreman returned again, this time to say they could not reach a majority verdict on my mother. The split was 9–3 in my favour and so the jury was hung. A hush fell over the courtroom and I felt my heart drop. It was a blow, but in truth I was not surprised. It was asking a lot of a group of complete strangers to

Maureen Wood

believe that a mother would do the unthinkable to her own child.

Mum's face made my skin crawl; she was smiling broadly, smugly, as though she had just won first prize. As though she had just got one over on me. Outside court, I met with my legal team.

'You're the only witness,' my barrister told me. 'Can you face a retrial? Can you face the whole thing again?'

He knew the stress had almost broken me and I think he was surprised by my instant answer. For me, there was no decision to make.

'Absolutely,' I said. 'Even if this finishes me off completely, I will see it through.'

I had to do it – I had come this far, and I had to see it through to the end. I felt she was the linchpin, the source of the evil. In my mind she was the catalyst for the abuse. She was my mother; she had been in a position to look after me. She could have taken me away from it all, she could have saved me. Instead, she joined in. There could be no worse betrayal, no more sickening treachery, than this.

After lunch we went back into court and the retrial was announced. This time Mum did not look quite so pleased with herself. She'd expected me to crumble after the first verdict. But she was wrong. I was finding a courage and a conviction that my family had never seen before. Next time, I realised, it would be just me and her. The mother of all trials, against the mother of all evil. And whilst a part of me dreaded it, I also looked forward

246

to it. This was my chance, my last chance, to set the record straight once and for all.

That September, John Wood and Jock were sentenced. In the morning, Louise collected me and drove me to court. Jock was in the foyer and we had no choice this time but to stand with him. It felt like a failing of the British justice system: abuser and abused, standing side by side.

'Make sure Mum gets what she deserves,' he said to me.

I didn't reply. John Wood, 68, was convicted of seven counts of rape and sentenced to sixteen years in prison. John Donnelly, 46, aka Jock Donnelly, received two years in jail after admitting rape, incest and indecent assault.

Again, my emotions were churning and contrary. I thought they should have got longer. Yet I also thought they'd got too long. Whilst I hated them for what they had done, I felt paralysed by the glaring fact that I had put my own brother and stepfather behind bars.

One month on, the day after my forty-first birthday, the retrial began. This time I had been counting down to the date. I wanted it to happen. But that first morning I had a panic attack. I felt like I was walking into a boxing ring, to fight my own mother. Me v Her. The only other witness was Marie, the police officer. Outside court, as I blew into a paper bag, people around me gave what they thought was well-meaning advice.

'She's a witch, she deserves it, you just need to be strong.'

'She's the last one, this is the last chapter. You've come this far, you can finish it now.'

But for me it was not so simple. This was my mother. The woman had carried me and given birth to me. Yes, she had abused me. Yes, she had betrayed me. But she had also cooked my meals, washed my clothes, put plasters on my grazed knees. She had called the radio when I was small, with a birthday dedication. She had helped me decorate my first home. She had been a grandmother, of sorts, to my children. Could I really condemn her? I was on the last mile of the marathon and yet I was ready to give up and limp home.

'I can't do it,' I said eventually. 'I'm sorry.'

My barrister asked the judge to give me one day's grace, to go home and make a decision, and he agreed. The next day, the trial would either go ahead or it would be abandoned for good. I had twenty-four hours to pull myself together. But I didn't think for a moment I'd be going back there. I felt as though I had been kidding myself, building myself up to a big 'one on one' battle with my mother, as though it was some sort of public straightener. An extravaganza of justice. Deep down, I was still a frightened little girl. I could not fight her. I would rather have faced anyone but her. She had given me life, and I felt sure, in that moment, that she would be the one to end it too.

Mick had the younger children for the day, so the

house was quiet. I lay in my bed and sobbed and sobbed. I knew that if the trial went ahead Mum's barrister would rip me to pieces again. Second time around it seemed even worse, because I knew what to expect. I knew how destructive it would be. I wasn't sure I could weather this storm. That night, as I lay in bed, tormented and confused, I heard Christopher's voice in my head, as clear as if he was perching on the edge of my duvet.

'*You can do it*,' he said. '*Course you can. You've been through worse than this. Much worse. And this time you have six children who believe in you.*

'*Six reasons to feel loved. Six reasons to feel proud.*

'*You're not on your own in that courtroom. I am with you, always.*'

His words brought me a sense of peace and I slept soundly, knowing that my boy had my back. The following morning I was outside the courtroom, bright and early. My barrister was delighted.

'I wasn't sure you would come back today,' he smiled.

'Neither was I,' I grinned. 'Let's just say I had a pep talk.'

As I took the stand I prepared myself for the onslaught. It was every bit as bruising as I had feared. Mum's barrister kept on referring to 'the sex with your brother'.

I bristled.

'Please don't say that,' I retorted. 'I did not have sex with him. I was a child. I was raped.'

The judge agreed with me.

'Please don't use that term again,' he instructed.

It was a scrap of comfort and it gave me a little bit of confidence.

'Would you not agree that you're unstable?' the barrister pressed. 'And that you fabricated the entire story?'

I knew he was trying to discredit me. It was my word against hers. That was all it came down to. For her part, Mum fell ill again when she was being cross-examined. She asked for an ambulance, but this time the judge called a doctor into court and he could find nothing obvious wrong with her. The trial continued and I allowed myself another small smile of satisfaction.

'*See?*' Christopher whispered. '*Things are going our way, Mum. Things are moving in our favour.*'

The jury went out, and I had the feeling, familiar by now, of time being on hold. I felt as though I was suspended in space. It was 4.30 p.m. the following day when the jury came back. I stayed in the witness room. I didn't expect a guilty verdict, I didn't dare hope that it might go my way. But I didn't regret it either. I could at least tell myself, and my children, that I had tried. I pushed all the way for justice and I had done everything I could to expose the truth. I had given it my all. But then, to my amazement, there was a bang on the door of the witness room and a voice shouted: 'Guilty!'

Outside, there was celebrating. The legal team were whooping and punching the air. And rightly so, for they had done a great job. For me, there was nothing like that. I felt, if anything, deflated. I felt no glee, no sense of victory. Mum was sentenced there and then. Aged 65, she was found guilty of four counts of aiding and abetting the rape of a girl under sixteen. She was jailed for nine years. I was told she had kept her 'pan face' even throughout the verdicts. I would never know whether she had any genuine regret or remorse. That day I handed back the shame, the disgust, the guilt and the pain. I dumped the lot on her. I was done with it. I had waited over thirty years for justice, thirty years to put my own family in prison. There were no winners. But now, at last, I could move on with my head held high.

When I got home, the kids crowded around with hugs and congratulations.

'Well done, Mum,' they said. 'You didn't give up.'

And a soft voice in my ear added: '*I knew you wouldn't. I had faith in you all the way, Mum.*'

Deep down, I was satisfied, though I didn't want to celebrate or make a big deal out of the verdicts. But that same week, SAIVE, the organisation that had provided my counselling, asked me to speak to the local paper.

'You're one of our success stories,' Louise explained. 'We hope we can persuade other people to come forward and get help.'

I agreed immediately. Louise had done so much for me, and if I could help in return I was more than happy to do so. I had no reservations at all about being identified publicly. I had kept silent for so many years that now

I wanted the world to know my story. I had a message to share, too. I wanted people to understand that women could also be abusers. That abuse came from all corners of society. And that hiding it and burying it was never the right thing to do. Mothers could be monsters, too. It was not a fashionable message, or a particularly pleasant one. It was hard to swallow. But it was pivotal that I spoke out.

When the paper came out, in January 2012, I was on the front page, with my photo, and I felt liberated. Local people were supportive. My friends were brilliant. One day I went into a bookshop and the assistant said: 'Well done. I saw you in the paper. You should write a book!'

'Maybe I will,' I replied. 'One step at a time.'

The only retaliation came, sadly, from my own wider family, from relatives of my mother. They were horrified at what they saw as me dragging the family name through the mud.

'This could have been sorted out, in the family, without the police,' said one.

'You should have let sleeping dogs lie,' said another.

I wasn't surprised. I was used to this sort of warped reaction from my relatives. But it was a bit disappointing, all the same. And a small piece of me was still afraid of them. A part of me still craved their acceptance and affection, even though I knew it would never come. Jock's house came under attack from vandals, with 'Paedo' daubed in paint across his walls. But I heard that his family were sticking by him. Despite everything.

A Family Secret

I joined Survivor groups on Facebook. I met people who were at breaking point from abuse, as I once had been. It was good to feel that I could help a little, that something positive could come from my own personal horror. I went to rallies, too – against sexual abuse and exploitation. And this new me felt good. This was better, so much better, than hiding everything away. My children recognised a huge change in me.

'You're happier in yourself, Mum,' Naomi told me. 'The shadow has gone from your eyes.'

In 2013 I was diagnosed with psoriatic arthritis, which, my doctor said, had been triggered by the stress of the past few years. There were days when I could barely move, and I needed a walking stick just to get around the house. One time I got stuck in the bath and could not get out and had to shout for my children to pull me up. It was a humiliating moment, but we managed to laugh about it, and Ben and Josh kept their eyes tightly closed!

'We've been through worse than this,' Ben giggled.

He was right. We had been through much worse. The hospital gave me a walking frame, but I was determined not to use it. It was a debilitating illness, but I wanted to learn to live with it. I was only forty-three years old, and I felt, in many ways, as though my life was just starting. When my psoriasis flared I was covered with ugly, weeping blisters and sores and I was in and out of hospital. But at home, life was reassuringly normal, and I was back to refereeing over arguments between the kids, clearing away breakfast pots and cooking Sunday dinners. It was predictable and boring and happy. It was everything I had always craved.

On 10 March 2014 there was a knock on my door.

'I'm from victim liaison –' said a strange woman on my doorstep.

'Which one is dead?' I interrupted.

She looked slightly taken aback at my bluntness and replied: 'Your mother.'

Now it was my turn to look shocked. For once, I was speechless. It had been a badly timed quip and I had not really expected her to reply. I felt as though I had been punched hard in the stomach and was badly winded.

'You'd better come inside,' I said.

She explained that Mum had undiagnosed cancer, in several places, but had actually died from a DVT. I had heard nothing since she was jailed and had not even known she was ill. She had been released from custody in Styal Women's Prison on compassionate grounds a few days earlier, and had died in Wythenshawe Hospital, Manchester.

'That's all the information I have,' said the liaison officer. 'I'm so sorry.'

'Don't be,' I said. 'But thank you for letting me know.'

I was taken aback that Mum was dead. I'd thought she was indestructible, that she would thunder on through life, barking out orders, bullying anyone who got in her way, and that she would easily outlive me. Nobody else had been notified of her passing because mine had been the only address the prison authorities had. I'd no idea even if anyone was with her when she died. John Wood was, of course, in prison himself. I had no contact with him or with any other relatives.

Reluctantly, I messaged family members and posted details of the funeral on Facebook. It was to be held at Macclesfield Crematorium, Cheshire, and was organised and paid for by the prison service. In a decision that I didn't quite understand myself, I went to the funeral. My children, except Ben, also wanted to attend. There were half a dozen other family members there too.

We walked from the train station to the crematorium, with no idea of what to expect or who we would see. Jock did not attend, and John Wood was not allowed to go from prison, because I was there. I had stopped him attending his own wife's funeral, and I was quite sure I would be castigated for that, along with everything else. Somehow he would blame me for that. Just before the service one of the mourners said to me: 'The feeling is that if you'd dealt with this in the family, she would not be dead. You destroyed her.'

I was stunned.

'But we had no family,' I protested. 'That was the whole problem.'

Even so, the guilt ate away at me. No matter what she had done, I didn't want her death on my conscience. Mum's other relatives ignored me completely, as though I was a bad smell. As though I was the problem. During the service the vicar read letters from fellow prisoners, saying what a lovely lady Mum was. I felt as though I was in a parallel universe, like I was starring in a bad movie.

How could a woman who abused her own daughter be a lovely lady? And why was Mum's family on her side, and not mine? Once again, all the old insecurities and misgivings of my childhood threatened to worm their way back into my consciousness, shaking the foundations of the new life I had built for me and the children.

'*Don't listen to them,*' Christopher said quietly, as the vicar said a final prayer. '*They don't know what they're talking about.*'

His words were a comfort, but I missed him sorely. As at any funeral, my thoughts were with him. As I watched the curtains close around Mum's coffin, I shuddered. It was a fitting end for a monster like her, to burn in the fires of hell. And I yet I felt no sense of revenge or satisfaction. Outside the crematorium I broke down, sobbing. I felt again as though it was all my fault. I had put her in prison. I had ruined her reputation. Maybe I had signed her death warrant, after all.

'*No,*' whispered Christopher. '*She signed it herself.*'

Chapter 15

After the court case I was advised to apply to the Criminal Injuries Compensation Authority and was told I would be entitled to a modest sum. I reckoned it would be enough to take the kids away for a week, maybe even go abroad for the first time. Money did not entrance me, it never had, but I wanted to give the children a treat.

From there I was directed to a firm of solicitors, to look further into the involvement of social services in my childhood. Marie's revelation at the trial had stuck in my mind. And in my throat, too. The idea, even the mere suggestion, that my abuse could have been stopped by social services left me cold with fury. It felt like my life had been not stolen, but handed willingly to my abusers. I instructed solicitors, based in Islington, London, to represent me.

'These matters are never straightforward, Maureen,' they warned. 'But we will do what we can.'

They discovered, as I suspected, that social services had been involved in my family life a lot over the years. In addition to the occasions I had remembered, there was also a time where a neighbour had made a report about us. Afterwards, I dimly recalled Mum going to the door and screaming threats at the street, as she tried to find out which neighbour had betrayed her.

'I'll kill them,' she had shouted.

Everything was slotting into place. I learned also that Mum herself had made a malicious report to social services about an elderly neighbour who she claimed was abusing me. There was an old man on our street and I would often walk his dog. I was about eleven years old, and I was studying World War Two at school. He would tell me fascinating stories about living through the war and fighting for his country; he brought the lessons alive, right there in his living room. He was a lovely old man, kind and gentle, and I thought of him as the grandad I had never had. Looking back, I think he probably felt sorry for me. He was my escape from the misery at home. He certainly had never laid a finger on me. But Mum had reported him to social services, probably, I think, as the fall guy in her plan. She was most likely covering herself for any revelations I might make in the future about her and John Wood. It was almost as though she was paving the way to head off the complaints before they were even made. She was a conniving and a lying woman and it was entirely possible that she had manipulated events to suit her, without a thought for our poor old neighbour. Or perhaps she was worried about me confiding in the old man and telling him about the abuse at home. Maybe she wanted him discredited and out of the way. Or – and this is quite likely – she was just a sick and twisted individual who could not believe that an elderly man and a young girl could share a genuine and innocent bond.

Either way, social services had got involved at her request, and I had to be interviewed and examined. I remembered a lady had asked if he was abusing me and I replied: 'No.' Again, nobody asked me the right question. Nobody asked me what was happening at home. Nobody asked if I was being abused by my brother, or my mother, or my stepfather. And I could not find the words without help. I so desperately needed help. There had been so many red flags over the years, so many alarm bells ringing so loudly that the social workers must have heard them. Added to that, social services knew Jock was abusing someone. They knew there was a victim. And even though I was pregnant at thirteen, they never thought to ask if it was me.

'Why did nobody join the dots?' I asked. 'Why did nobody care about me?'

I wanted an apology from social services. I could and should have been removed and protected. My solicitors agreed, and a legal action was launched. But the investigation was slow and difficult. Social services struggled to find the files from my childhood and it dragged on and on. I had to see two psychiatrists, one for each side, and

Maureen Wood

Naomi came with me to the appointments. I hated dredging the past up yet again, but I was adamant that someone had to be held to account. I wanted to make sure that other kids were better protected in the future and that nobody else fell through the net and was trampled underfoot, as I had been. And for me, having survived three criminal trials and the ruthlessness of the barristers, an interview with a shrink really was a walk in the park! One day in November 2015, as I waited in my solicitors' office, there were phone calls flying back and forth between the two sides. I had no real idea what was happening or what kind of settlement they were discussing.

At the end of it my solicitor said: 'We've settled out of court, Maureen. We hope you'll be pleased with the offer. We certainly think you will.'

I was awarded an eyewatering £200,000 from Staffordshire County Council. I was astonished at the figure. I had only ever wanted someone to admit they were wrong, but I couldn't deny that the money was a huge bonus. I couldn't deny that I was absolutely thrilled.

'Thank you,' I beamed.

All through raising my children I'd scrimped and saved. I'd struggled even to pay for a weekend in Wales. With the Criminal Injuries pay-out, I had hoped, perhaps, to take them to Europe on a package holiday – Spain or maybe Portugal. But I had always promised them, always, that if I ever came into money we would go to America. It was a standing joke in our family. Ever since they had been toddlers we'd sat and drooled over Disney brochures, admiring the theme parks, and playing make-believe.

'Shall we go there?' Naomi would say, pointing to hotels with Disney characters waving outside. 'Or there?'

Whenever I had a bunch of ten-pound notes the kids would wave them and shout: 'We're off to America! See you next week!'

It was a pipe dream. A flight of fancy. Nothing more. Now, that was all about to change. I took the train home from London in a complete daze, grinning from ear to ear. Back at home, I sat my children down in the living room to give them the good news in person. As they took their seats, I noticed Michaela was wide-eyed and hesitant.

'What is it, Mum?' she asked.

Her words pulled on my heartstrings. They were so used to me sharing bad news, worrying news, traumatic news. The past few years had brought one crushing blow after another for my family.

But now we were on the up. Now, at last, it was our turn to enjoy life.

'We're going to Disneyland!' I yelled suddenly, throwing my arms around them. 'It's time to spend, spend, spend!'

We all ended up in a big hug, laughing and crying all at once. By Christmas I got the first instalment of my settlement and I had £90,000 in my bank account. My eyes goggled when I saw the balance at the cash point. It almost frightened me; the sheer responsibility of such a large amount of cash. Of course, I knew I should be sensible and save my money. I knew I should invest it, maybe in a property or in shares. I should be frugal and careful and measured in my approach. But I also knew that life was too short, and that my children had suffered too much. Now was the time to relax and have fun, without the shadow that had weighed on us for so long.

'Sod it,' I grinned. 'We will spend the lot!'

We had a blast that Christmas. I took the kids shopping and told them to buy whatever they fancied. They got new clothes, headphones, mobile phones and laptops. All top spec, all the best brands. These were things we'd never been able to afford until now. It was a far cry from that Christmas shopping trip where I had struggled to afford pyjamas from Primark, where I'd cowered from my mum in the street, like a frightened animal. In the New Year I refurbished the entire house. I bought a new sofa and chairs, beautiful solid oak drawers, new beds and a new bathroom suite. I picked out curtains and cushions, rugs and bedding. I chose new lights and lamps and picture frames.

'What about this? Or this? Or this?' Naomi asked.

'Let's buy the bloody lot,' I replied. 'Why not?'

We found ourselves laughing hysterically, just at the sheer unfeasibility of the situation. Everything, my entire life, had been second-hand, passed on from well-meaning friends or from charity shops. For the first time it was all brand spanking new. Everything shone.

A Family Secret

Everything gleamed. I snapped off the price tags and beamed. My gift to myself was an Aga cooker with a double oven. I'd spent years cooking Christmas dinners for my whole family with one oven. I juggled five pans on four rings and had to jam the Yorkshires and the roasties in around the turkey. I had cursed my oven over the years, so many times. We had a love-hate relationship, for, though I loved to cook, it was too small and way past its best. I'd had to make do for many years. But no longer. This, for me, was unlimited luxury. I felt like Mary Berry herself. The day it arrived I cooked up a big roast dinner for the entire family, just because I could.

'This is great, Mum,' smiled my children. 'Really great.'

By now, Ben had his own flat, as did Josh, and both lived near to me. I bought them white goods for their kitchens and some furniture. I loved being able to help them. People might say I wasted my money. I would disagree. There was no price for the smile on my kids' faces. The feeling of being able to assist them, to set them up in life, was brilliant. When the next instalment of the compensation arrived I went straight out to my local branch of Co-op travel and told the agent exactly what I wanted. I had been planning it for long enough after all!

'I'd like a month in Florida please,' I said. 'First-class travel.'

I booked two weeks at the Swan and Dolphin Resort at Walt Disney World, with tickets for the parks and a day swimming with dolphins. Then I requested a further two weeks at the Hard Rock Hotel at Universal Studios. The entire trip came to a staggering £35,000. The travel agent's jaw almost hit the desk. I couldn't blame him. I was still in shock myself.

'It's a long story,' I told him with a smile. 'Let's just say me and my kids deserve a break.'

We started shopping for our trip, buying summer clothes, sun hats and swimwear. We had never flown before. The children had never even been abroad. And apart from the first few months of my life in Germany, on an army base, neither had I. We didn't even have passports, and I had to apply for the lot. We all had to have interviews, except Michaela, who was still a child. Mine was tricky, as I had no idea of my father's date of birth. I couldn't find his birth certificate, despite searching online. Eventually I traced it back from his marriage certificate, but it took weeks of detective work and anxious worry before my passport application could be approved. Our holiday was booked for August 2016 and the kids were dizzy with excitement. And I was the biggest kid of all!

'I can't wait, I can't wait!' I kept saying.

We went down to Heathrow two days early, to an airport hotel, to get ourselves into the holiday spirit. On the day of the flight we were ushered into the first-class lounge, where we were waited on hand and foot. I was the one who was used to waiting on everyone else, and this was a welcome change. I was offered a cooked breakfast, and champagne!

A Family Secret

'Wow,' I gasped, unable to stop beaming.

I had never known anything like it, and we were still in the airport! I swapped my champagne discreetly for an orange juice and raised a toast along with my children.

'To Christopher,' I said. 'Always in our hearts.'

'*I am always with you,*' he whispered. '*You know that by now, Mum.*'

I was nervous about flying, but then, as we boarded, I spotted the name of the plane: Tinkerbell, which was my nickname for Michaela. It felt like a sign from Christopher. And it was enough to ease my nerves. We settled ourselves in first class, like royalty, and sat back to enjoy the journey. The flight went like a dream but up there, in the clouds, I couldn't help thinking of my first-born, of my little angel, who had made all of this happen. For a little boy who had lived only three weeks, his impact had been quite breathtaking.

'Thank you, son,' I said softly.

When we arrived, the hotel was fantastic, it was everything we had dreamed of and more. We had two rooms – one for the boys, one for the girls. And every day we had a ball. My arthritis was playing up, and some days I stayed by the pool whilst the kids went off to the theme parks. But I wasn't complaining. Money even helped with pain! My psoriasis cleared up with the sunshine, too. We rode rollercoasters, swam with dolphins and ate burgers as big as dinner plates.

'Can we live here forever?' Michaela asked.

Maureen Wood

When the month was up, we all cried. We didn't want to come home at all. I could have stayed there for another month, quite easily. I felt on top of the world, spending time with my children, spoiling them in ways I had never imagined possible. Later that year, the money ran out. I had blown the lot on holidays, treats and renovating my home. Yet I didn't miss it. In my opinion it had been very well spent. People have often asked since if I regret it, if I wish I had made an investment instead. That always makes me smile, because for me the memory of that holiday, the time with my children, the laughs we had shared … now that was the wisest investment of all.

Epilogue

And so while my life was reaching new heights of euphoria, what became of the people who had tried to destroy it? The date 6 September 2012 was marked on my mental calendar and ingrained in my mind. I had been in court when the judge said that Jock would serve exactly twelve months in prison, so I knew his release date and it might as well have been tattooed onto my memory. The day came around and I was strangely jittery and afraid, as though he might come straight from prison to give me a piece of his mind – or worse. I remembered another surprise visit he'd made to my house:

'Fancy one for old times' sake?'

Even now the memory repulsed and enraged me. And a small part of me, though I did not want to admit it, was still very frightened of him. That day I kept both front and back door locked, and I carried my mobile phone from room to room. I could not shake a sense of impending doom. As it happened, I heard nothing. The day passed just like any other. And I didn't even get the letter that he was being released until three weeks after the event. It felt a bit like the day Mum had walked past me as I was Christmas shopping at Primark. There had been a huge build-up that had simply petered out, into nothing.

That December, three months after his release, I thought that I saw Jock at the Christmas lights switch-on in Stoke, I felt sure it was him, striding past me in the dark. I couldn't be absolutely certain, it was gloomy and drizzly and his head was down. But I would know that walk anywhere. And again, like the Christmas shopping trip, it floored me and left me reeling.

'I'm heading home, I've got a headache,' I told my kids.

I scurried away with a sick feeling in my stomach. I didn't want any reminders. I heard later that Jock still lived in the city and so I was always careful to avoid his area. I wasn't living in fear of him, but neither did I want a show-down. Over six years later, in February 2019, I got a letter informing me that John Wood would soon be up for release and asking me for my response. I had so many churning through my mind that I really didn't know where to start.

'Please don't let him live anywhere near me,' I wrote back. 'I don't want to see him.'

In the weeks that followed, I was plagued by night-mares and flashbacks. I could see John Wood, stroking his goatee beard, fixing me with his watery stare, threatening me with his cold voice.

'Tell anyone and I'll kill you. I'll kill you, Maureen.'

But these were not on the scale of the nightmares before the trial and I knew they never would be. The horror was still there and it always would be, but I had learned that talking helped to dilute it. Getting my memories out of the locked box, and setting them free, had not only secured justice but had also helped me to cope. I had been set free myself as a result. John Wood was released from prison in April 2019, and soon after, a friend called in to see me.

'He's living around five minutes away from you,' she confided. 'I've seen him going in and out of his house.'

It was a spine-chilling thought. I wished desperately that it could be further away, and I felt angry that it wasn't. But I was also determined not to be cowed by him. I had lived in fear for most of my life and I was not prepared to go back to that. One day, Ben came home to tell me he had spotted John Wood whilst he was out shopping.

'Honestly, Mum, it was all I could do not to go over there and shout in his face,' he said. 'I wanted to kill him, to hurt him the way he has hurt you and all of us.'

But in the end Ben had shown great dignity and simply walked past with his head held high. I was so proud of him.

'You're a good man,' I told Ben with a smile.

Maureen Wood

Three months later, Mick, my ex, sadly died at the age of 67. He had suffered a catastrophic brain bleed. He was the children's father, and we'd shared some great times together. I knew I would miss him, especially at Christmas, which we had always shared as a family. He had been brilliant throughout the court cases, too.

The months have passed and I've not bumped into John Wood or Jock yet, but in truth I do avoid going into the city centre, and around the areas where I know they live. I like to think that if I ever saw them I would be brave and confrontational and I would hold them to account. But the more realistic part of me thinks I would run away and panic. I don't ever want to find out. I've done my bit, after all, in bringing them to justice. And I don't need any more reminders. If I never see them again it will be far too soon. I am trying, and I will always try, to spend less time thinking about them and concentrating more on the future. My next project is to study sociology and psychology through the Open University. I'd like to help other survivors of abuse. Like Mary, like Louise, I want to be there for people who have completely given up on themselves. I think I understand a little of what it means to feel utterly abandoned. And I'd like to pass on that experience.

Right from being a little girl, I objected to sharing a name with my mother. She, like me, was Maureen Wood. I'd see her name on letters, and shudder. I hated that our names connected us. Did that make me the same as her, I used to wonder? Did that mean I was cruel and wicked and heartless? Would I grow up to be violent and deranged too? As I grew older, I resented it even more. I didn't want to be a part of her family and I certainly didn't want her name. In court, when I heard her name called out, it made me cringe. We were on opposite sides. She the abuser, me the abused. I wanted justice and truth. She wanted secrets and lies. So why should we share the same name? And at her funeral, too, when I saw her name on the coffin, I baulked. I no longer wanted any association with her. I loathed everything she had stood for. When the coffin moved into the furnace, I imagined the plaque burning in the flames, and for me it was a fitting end for the name. I wanted no more association with Maureen Wood.

'Good riddance,' I told myself.

There was no maternal bond. I doubt she even under-stood what that meant. Yet we were bound together. I was manacled, like a slave, to the woman I despised more than anyone else in the world, to the woman who had betrayed me and snared me and abandoned me to evil.

'No more,' I said firmly.

And so I decided to take control, and to change my name.

'But to what?' I wondered.

I could have chosen Donnelly, after my birth father, but he had done nothing at all for me. I honestly wouldn't have recognised him if I'd met him in the street. It seemed ridiculous to choose his name; we had no real connection. But naturally, one name sprung to my mind.

'Johnson,' I said, with a smile.

And I heard a little voice, at my shoulder, saying:

'*Yes, Mum, that's a lovely idea.*'

My bond with Mary was precious; visceral and real. She wasn't a blood relative; no, it was stronger, much stronger, than that. Our relationship had grown and flourished, not through genes, but in our hearts. Mary had put up with my teenage strops during that first year of counselling. I'd been a grade A pain in the arse, desperate to push her away, but it hadn't worked. She hung in there. She had brought me a cooker when I got my first place, and a bed for Ben, too. She'd been round with polish and a duster. Other times, she'd brought me a bag of shopping. She was my shoulder to cry on and she was my kick up the backside when I needed it too. She was quiet and calm and a constant support. To my children, she was Aunty Mary. To me, she was a surrogate mother. Secretly, as a young mum, I used to wish that Mary was my real mother. I remembered one occasion vividly, a meeting at the Christian fellowship, and Mary had invited me along. She was there with her own daughters. As I watched them, with their easy, unconditional relationship and their small signs of affection, I felt a surge of jealousy. I wanted that. I wanted what they had. Mary was incredibly intuitive and she recognised what I was feeling.

A Family Secret

'I realised that day that I wanted to do more for you, to be someone for you,' she confided.

The maternal relationship was there, far deeper than it could ever have been with my own mother. After I went to the police, Mary was a daily support. And when my children lost their own grandparents, after I told them about the abuse, Mary became their Nanna instead. She just slotted into the role. It was their choice. And for Mary, it felt like an honour. So I began using Johnson as my surname. It was just on social media at first, but as time went on I started using it day to day too. I liked the sound of it. I liked the way it looked on letters. It was another step towards the new me, another piece of the jigsaw to making me whole.

Next, I decided to drop Maureen. Maureen, Dozy-Mozy, Mo-Jo; I hated them all. The names stuck in my throat and made me gag. To me, Maureen was vicious. She was cruel. She was my mother. She was everything I didn't want to be. I began calling myself Tori instead. Tori is short for Victorious and needs no more explanation. For me, smiling and surviving, and having the love of my children, is the biggest victory of all.

I feel so blessed despite what I have suffered, because my children have supported me every step of the way. I have many regrets that I let my kids down at times. I am not the perfect mother, but I am always trying to improve. I'm not in a relationship and haven't had a serious partner since Josie, all those years ago. I haven't given up on love, but I do accept that perhaps I'm not cut out for long-term commitments. And now, at nearly fifty years of age, that really doesn't bother me one bit. My life is all about my kids – and their kids, too. I have three little granddaughters now, who bring me so much happiness and keep me on my toes. The last word must go to my eldest son, Christopher, my guardian angel who saved my life not once, but twice. He taught me how to love and how to be strong. I can feel him here today, with me, guiding me through life.

'*Well done, Mum, well done, I love you.*'

His light shines on.

Acknowledgements

I would like to thank my children for their unwavering support during the whole process of fighting for justice and then while doing this book.

Hilda Hollinshead, for being my substitute mum. You have always supported me throughout every step of my journey since we first met as counsellor and client in 1990. I would not be the person I am today without your influence. Also Jack Hollinshead, for being my substitute dad.

Sue Sharp, for being my sounding board and confidante. You were there for me during my darkest days, and I shall be eternally grateful.

Janet Coope, thank you for believing in me and restoring my faith in the police and the British justice system.

My writers Joe and Ann Cusack, thank you for all the hard work that you both put in to get this book together for me; and to Joe, for being persistent – it only took you eight years of waiting until I was ready to do this.

Maureen Wood

To Kelly Ellis and her team at HarperCollins, thank you for taking my book on and for all the hard work you have put in to get it to a finished product.

And finally thank you to Kevin Pocklington at the North Literacy Agency.

MOVING
Memoirs

Stories of hope, courage and
the power of love . . .

Sign up to the Moving Memoirs email and you'll
be the first to hear about new books, discounts,
and get sneak previews from your
favourite authors!

Sign up at

www.moving-memoirs.com

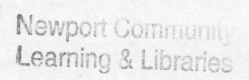